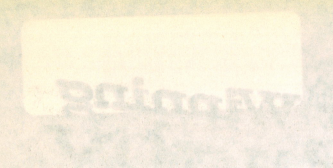

Think & Play Winning Rugby

Hugh de Lacy with Grant Fox

An imprint of HarperCollins*Publishers*

*The authors gratefully acknowledge the assistance of
Dr David Whitehead of Christchurch, New Zealand,
in preparing the section on mind-control of pain.*

Harper*Sports*
An imprint of HarperCollins*Publishers*

First published 2000
HarperCollins*Publishers (New Zealand) Limited*
P.O. Box 1, Auckland

Copyright © Hugh de Lacy and Grant Fox 2000
Photographs copyright © Peter Bush 2000

Hugh de Lacy and Grant Fox assert the moral right to be identified as the authors of this work.

All rights reserved. No part of this publication may be reproduced, stored in a retrieval system or transmitted in any form or by any means, electronic, mechanical, photocopying, recording or otherwise, without the prior written permission of the publishers.

ISBN 1 86950 338 4

Designed and typeset by Graeme Leather
Printed by Griffin Press, Netley on 79 gsm Bulky Paperback

Contents

Introduction	7
1. Meet Siggy, the blinkered whizz-kid	**17**
Practising awareness	19
Accumulating accurate data	25
2. Meet Napoleon, the temperamental emperor	**28**
3. The art of concentration	**37**
4. The snowball effect	**45**
5. Goal-setting	**51**
6. Goals	**59**
The golden rules of goal-setting	60
Defining your goals	63
7. Affirmations	**77**
How to write affirmations	80
8. Creative visualisation	**84**
Play-by-play use of creative visualisation	87
9. Relaxation techniques	**91**
Muscular control	93
Brain-wave control	95
Breathing meditation	97
Transcendental meditation	97
Autogenic training	98
10. Anchoring	**101**
The supercharger	104
11. Peak experiences	**106**
The expectation index	110
The hometown syndrome	115

12. The grand paradox meets the Grant Fox place kick   120
    The Grant Fox place-kicking ritual   125
    Kicking in the wind   134
    The step-kick exercise   136

13. Harnessing fear, managing pain   138
    Fear   140
    Pain   142

14. Playing the mind game   148
    The backs   150
    The forwards   154

15. Of gamesmanship and things . . .   158
    Sportsmanship   165

Introduction

From the day rugby was first played in New Zealand (on 14 May 1870), the game struck a chord in the hearts of New Zealanders. There was something about the combination of skill, physicality and teamwork that both the British colonials and the indigenous Maori took to with relish. It was probably no coincidence that both cultures had long histories of sophisticated warfare, and that they were at war with each other over land at the time. The outcome of the New Zealand land wars of the 1860s and 1870s was indecisive, but there was no denying the impact of rugby on both peoples, and the contribution it made to their learning to live together in relative harmony thereafter.

The warrior culture at New Zealand's heart never died—its energies were just channelled into a sport that contains the same elements of physical risk, commitment and achievement, but without the death, destruction and victimisation of innocents that is the inevitable accompaniment of warfare.

From the time the first New Zealand rugby team toured overseas in 1884, winning eight games out of eight, this tiny South Pacific country, whose population today is still under four million, has been a dominant force in the game. It is New Zealand's national sport, and no other sport has the capacity to galvanise the nation as rugby does.

With the advent of professionalism in the last few years, New Zealand's influence has spread worldwide, with New Zealanders showing up as coaches of Wales (Graham Henry), Ireland (Warren Gatland), England (John Mitchell), Samoa (Bryan Williams), Fiji and now Italy (Brad Johnstone) and Argentina (Alex Wyllie).

In the days leading up to the 1999 World Cup, to decide who would carry the mantle of international rugby supremacy into the new millennium, speculation about the outcome focused on two New Zealand coaches in particular: John Hart, in charge of New Zealand's All Blacks; and Graham Henry, who had wrought a spectacular revival of Welsh rugby, the highlight of which was Wales' first-ever win over the South African Springboks in a century of trying.

John Hart and Graham Henry have two things in common: they both coached Auckland sides during an extended period of dominance of New Zealand provincial and professional rugby; and they both relied on Grant Fox to be the general who masterminded that dominance on the pitch.

Probably no other single player has had as great an impact on the New Zealand game as Fox has had—certainly no other has scored as many points for New Zealand. And no other player is as qualified as Grant Fox, in terms both of experience and his own analytical and clinical approach to the game, to isolate and identify the mental factors that make the differences between a player, a good player, and a great player.

By the time you step out onto the pitch to play full-contact, 80-minute rugby, you've already made a serious investment in physical training, in terms of both time and effort, on your own and with the team. So what a waste it is if you then fail to get the best out of yourself. Where's the enjoyment in playing if, at the end of the game, you come away feeling you could have done better, if only...? What's the point of playing to only part of your potential? Is it really only an outstanding few players who can perform to their best every time they take the field? Or is such consistency and excellence within the reach of all of us—if we only knew how?

Most players manage to really hit their straps only once or twice a season, and the memories of those special matches stay with them for years. Think of your own best games—of your whole career or just of the past season—and how you walked off after the match, physically wasted but mentally buzzing, and savoured the satisfaction with your team-mates in the club-rooms afterwards.

Wouldn't it be great if you could come off the field feeling *that* satisfied with your performance *every* time you played, win or lose? It would make all those hours of training and practice worth so much more.

So how come you don't? How come these peak performances seem to occur more by accident than design?

The first thing to understand is that satisfaction with your performance—or lack of it—exists in only one place: your mind. And if *you* aren't satisfied in your own mind with your performance, you can't expect anyone else—your team-mates, the coach, selectors—to be satisfied with it either. The key factor in delivering peak performances, in getting the greatest possible satisfaction out of your investment in training and time, is the state of your mind before, during and after the game.

Which leads us to the next question: how do you condition your mind so that your body delivers a peak performance—realises your full potential—every time you want it to?

The answers, as Grant Fox studied and practised them, are in this book.

Because it involves stamina and contact as well as skill, rugby demands physical fitness as a basic prerequisite—otherwise you can't keep up with the play and you get injured in the physical stuff. At its highest level, rugby is for those in the prime of their lives who have also prepared themselves over months and years to a highly specialised and advanced level of fitness and skills. Even social and Golden Oldies rugby require a basic level of physical fitness, as the toll of injury and heart attack among the unfit attests.

But being the physically fittest and most skilled player in the team is no guarantee of being the most useful on the field on the day. Examples abound of physically fit and individually skilled teams that never win games, and of amazingly fit and proficient players who never get selected for better teams.

On the other hand, there are just as many examples of players and teams whose physical preparation is notoriously shoddy, or whose skills and co-ordination are inferior, but who rise to the occasion week after week to beat fitter and more skilled sides.

How come? What's that key ingredient that makes the difference between a competition-winning team and an also-ran? Motivation?

In part, yes, but motivation to win varies with the circumstances of every game. Is it a championship match before the provincial or national selectors, or a minor club game with nothing much at stake? In the end, motivation is just another word for desperation: if you're desperate enough to win, you're motivated enough. So motivation isn't the complete answer—in fact it's just one part of a winning formula, in the same way that petrol is part of a winning racing car.

However you define it, whatever you want to call the winning formula, it comes down to this—winning rugby requires a combination of physical fitness and skill, *plus mental fitness*.

If you have two teams of equal physical fitness and skill, the one that will win is the one that is better trained mentally. To that extent, rugby is a mind-game. And to get good at it, you have to train your mind.

Just like physical fitness, mental fitness is a product of training—mental training. Just like physical training, mental training is a deliberate and planned activity, designed to allow you, the rugby player, to perform to your potential on the field every time you want to or need to. And that's what this book is designed to do: to teach you how to train your mind to make the very most of the physical training that you have imposed on your body.

It needs to be emphasised here that mind-training in rugby can never be a total substitute for physical training. You still have to do the roadwork and the gymwork to play rugby at any level, because you have to condition your body to cope with the physical exertion and the body-contact.

But by the same token, in these days of professional rugby you can't make it to the top without some form of mental training that, consciously or unconsciously, at least equates in sophistication and planning to your physical preparation. It's fair to say that no elite international player stays at the top of the game without a form of mental training that is as thorough as their physical training. Some may not have known they were undergoing mental training until the sports psychologists—the team 'shrinks'—got hold of them and told them so. But long before they graduated to teams important enough to employ psychologists, they were training themselves mentally, whether they realised it or not.

In short, no matter how hard you train physically, you'll never get the best out of yourself unless you also train yourself mentally. Professional rugby has raised the standards of the game at every level to such a degree that you can't even think about performing to your potential unless you are as serious about mind-training as you are about body-training. And this book tells you how to train your mind.

This book is for the individual rugby player—it comes from an individual perspective, not a team perspective. It teaches you how to train your own mind so you perform better and get greater satisfaction from your game, whether or not anyone else in your team does the same. This book shows you how to complement your physical training with mental training so that, when you get out there on the field, the 80 minutes of rugby you deliver is the best 80 minutes you're capable of. This book tells you how to realise your potential as a rugby player, at whatever level you choose to play.

What the mind truly believes, the body inevitably delivers.

There, in nine words, is the key to understanding human performance in any field, be it body-building or budgie breeding, rocket science or rugby. Those nine words encompass all human behaviour. Above all, they access the single most important resource available to the person who loves their sport and wants to perform better at it: the resource of the mind. Yet among sportspeople in the Western world, full professionals aside, that's a resource they've barely begun to tap.

What the mind truly believes, the body inevitably delivers.

That statement explains the difference between excellence and mediocrity, between the champion and the also-ran, between winning and losing. The body that wins is guided—driven—by the mind that truly expects to win.

It seems so obvious, yet this is a concept that relatively few Western sportspeople have so far grasped. There's a huge amount of good, solid Western science devoted to the training of the human body for a vast range of highly specialised sports, rugby among them, yet the science of training the mind is still in its infancy in the West.

To some degree the physical training you have to put in for rugby also trains your mind: your motivation, for example, might grow as a result of the effort you put into physical preparation. Then again it might not: if your physical training is not rewarded by quality performances, the motivation to both train and perform withers away.

Motivation doesn't just happen like a run of luck—it's a skill in itself and, like any skill, it requires nurturing. You need to practise motivation, just as you need to practise kicking or tackling or passing.

Of course, the better you prepare physically, the better you'll play qualitatively—no one's arguing with that. But by the same token, any improvement in your physical condition raises your potential by the same degree: if you're twice as fit this year as you were last year, your potential is twice is high. The key question is: are you any closer to realising your potential this year than you were last year—or are you just a physically fitter under-performer?

The effect of physical training alone on mental fitness is haphazard, accidental—a matter of, yes, luck. You might find yourself turning on a blinder if everything leading up to the game goes your way. But you can just as easily be put off your game by all sorts of outside factors: the bus trip, the state of the pitch, hostile spectators, a bad-tempered referee, the colour of the changing-room walls.

All the physical training in the world offers no guarantee that you'll be able to deliver the goods on the day. And if you want to realise your full potential, whatever your degree of physical fitness, you've got to be mentally trained, mentally fit. Mental fitness is not a matter of good luck—it's a matter of good mental training.

Long before 1823, when William Webb Ellis first inspired the pupils and masters at Rugby Public School in England, by electing to carry the ball instead of just kicking it, many cultures—the Indians of Central America, the Celts of Western Europe—had developed pastimes based on the same simple principles: you carry a ball towards an opposing goal; your opponents try to stop you. The marvellous game that Ellis re-invented was taken to the furthest corners of the planet by the British colonists, spawning such derivations on the way as the human chess game in the United States they call gridiron.

Early in its history, rugby split between an amateur code—rugby union—and a professional one—rugby league. Now that rugby union has followed league into full professionalism, it's not outside the bounds of possibility that the two codes may eventually reunite. This book is aimed primarily at the union code, but there are enough similarities between the two for the principles described here to be applied successfully, with minor and obvious modifications, to league as well.

The legend of William Webb Ellis has it that he picked up the ball during a soccer match and ran with it out of frustration. In fact it wasn't a soccer match at all, but a local version of a scrummaging and mauling game played at many British private schools. Ellis's contribution was in demonstrating the greater appeal in carrying the ball over merely kicking it. Ellis couldn't have known that the idea would catch on so readily and make such an impact on such a wide range of countries and cultures, from the Celts and the Polynesians to the Latins and the Anglos, the Asians and the Africans.

Today, rugby union reaches its highest expression at the World Cup tournaments held every four years, and in the Six Nations (Five Nations until the addition of Italy in 2000) in the northern hemisphere, and the Super 12 in the southern. The shortened, high-speed version of the game, sevens, became a Commonwealth Games sport in 1998 (with New Zealand winning the first gold medal). There is also on-going debate about either sevens or the full version of the game becoming an Olympic sport. (The full version was played at the Olympics in the 1920s, with the United States winning the last Olympic rugby gold medal.)

But when young Bill Ellis ran with the ball in 1823, he couldn't have imagined what would become of the game he is credited with inventing. For all the sophistication of the game today, it still caters to the same basic human instincts—to run, to kick, to receive and carry and pass the ball, to tackle and to evade or break tackles—that motivated Ellis to break out of the restrictions that mere 'football' imposed on him.

Today men and women, girls and boys the world over respond to those same instincts as they take to rugby in rapidly increasingly numbers. Ellis's spontaneous act of rebellion has matured into their conscious decision to share the exhilaration of running and passing and tackling and kicking, and the inevitable risk inherent in the organised and controlled violence of physical contact. The risk is a key element in the game's magnetic attraction but, where Ellis entered into it without apparent prior thought, today's players do it on the basis of informed imagination and clarity of purpose. Today's players know what they're getting into (informed imagination), and they get into it specifically to experience the challenge and excitement of it (clarity of purpose).

And it's those two elements—informed imagination and clarity of purpose—taken to their highest forms that distinguish not just the very best rugby players from the mediocre, but the most satisfied and fulfilled rugby players from those who don't get as much out of the game as they'd like to. Satisfaction and fulfilment are, in the end, the ultimate goals of the rugby player. And, through mind-training, those goals are within the reach of all of us.

The principles and practices of mind-training described in this book were developed over years of trial and error in the relative isolation of New Zealand, and first written down in manuscript form by my brother, Mark de Lacy, who had applied them with notable success to the game of lawn bowls (using these principles Mark skipped a rink of supposed no-hopers all the way to a New Zealand championship final). That manuscript first saw the light of day in book form in 1992 in the first of the *Think & Play* series. Mark co-authored the book with double world lawn bowls champion, and fellow New Zealander, Peter Belliss. The significance of pioneering these techniques in the game of lawn bowls was that, unlike rugby, bowls has hardly any physical input: virtually anyone can play bowls, regardless of age, sex or physical condition. Because physique and physical fitness count for so little, bowls is the quintessential mind-game: to get good at it you have to train your mind. It doesn't really matter what sort of shape your body is in.

In rugby, of course, your physical condition matters a great deal—you've got to get physically fit to at least some degree to play the game at any level. But, as we discussed earlier, what distinguishes top, satisfied and fulfilled rugby players from run-of-the-mill, dissatisfied and frustrated ones is their mental attitude to the game. And getting the *right* mental attitude to rugby requires mental training, just as it does for lawn bowls or any other sport you care to name.

The basic principles that Mark de Lacy and Peter Belliss applied so successfully to lawn bowls are equally applicable to rugby—they just need to be modified to match the peculiar demands of the running-kicking-passing-tackling and physical contact game.

When it came to seeking a co-author to adapt those mind-training techniques to rugby, one person stood out among all other rugby personalities. Grant Fox is a singular figure within the pantheon of rugby greats, in part because he scored more points in international rugby than any other New Zealander, but even more than that, because he is remembered as the thinking person's rugby player. His concept of the game was never confined to the old stereotypes of forwards as cannon-fodder and backs as cavalry. Instead, he saw the wider picture, the meshing of each of the fifteen individual positions into a cohesive whole. And long before sports psychologists became vital members of all leading international rugby management teams, Fox understood and practised the principles of personal mental preparation that you will encounter in this book.

The net result is an approach to rugby that you will find to be stunningly effective. These techniques, made specific to rugby by the personal experience of Grant Fox, work because they're logical, simple, and geared specifically to the game. Fox and I guarantee they'll work for you.

These techniques can be summed up in those nine magical words: what the mind truly believes, the body inevitably delivers.

Or, to put it another way: *Think & Play Winning Rugby*.

Hugh de Lacy
Parnassus
North Canterbury
New Zealand

−1−
Meet Siggy,
the blinkered whizz-kid

> Most people live, whether physically, intellectually or morally, in a very restricted circle of their potential being. They make use of a very small portion of their possible consciousness, and of their soul's resources in general, much like a man who, out of his whole bodily organism, should get into the habit of using and moving only his little finger. Great emergencies and crises show us how much greater our vital resources are than we supposed. **WILLIAM JAMES**

In today's world of electronics and microchip technology, we've come to accept that computers can be designed and built to cope with almost any situation. Technology has advanced so quickly it would be silly of us to underestimate what man-made machines are capable of. Even 50 years ago, anyone predicting such standard appliances as mobile phones, microwave cookers and computer games would have been dismissed as loony. Yet all of these things are here, as common as sparrows, because some people realised that anything is possible once we begin to harness the most impressive and under-used power source at our disposal: the human brain.

So what's all this got to do with a recreational (or even professional) pastime like rugby football? The answer is that the breakthrough tool that produced these modern electronic marvels was the computer, and it was the human brain that provided the working model for it. So it can be fairly said that each of us possesses a super-powered personal in-built computer that is the most sophisticated and complex piece of matter, for its size, in the universe. To play better rugby all we have to do is to gear our personal super-computer to refine the skills and attitudes peculiar to the game.

Perhaps because it was supplied free, we tend not to appreciate our brain. Certainly, most of us at any time use only a small part of this incredible computer's huge capacity. The human brain is capable of working out with unerring accuracy, and in a fraction of a second, all the variables involved in striking an oval ball in such a way that it travels anything up to 60 metres to pass between a pair of goalposts 5.6 metres apart and over a horizontal crossbar 3 metres above the ground.

Grant Fox made a career out of doing this—and that's without taking into account the rest of the range of highly polished rugby skills that made him famous.

To do the same, all we need to do is feed our personal in-built computer with enough correct information, and it'll do everything else. But the thing about all computers—human as well as man-made—is that they produce the desired results only if the programmers have fed the correct data into them. Feed in faulty data and you get flawed results: 'garbage in, garbage out'. Similarly, our personal computers (our brains) will produce the desired results (accurate goal kicks, for example), but only if they have enough correct data fed in by their operators (us).

So, if we want to increase the percentage of goals we kick, we have to develop the habit of supplying our computer-brains with clear and accurate information. The same goes for all the other skills and judgements rugby involves. To supply clear and accurate information, we must practise awareness.

Once we've supplied this awareness-based information to our personal computers, we have to learn to trust them to produce the desired results. Garbled results (missed kicks, dropped passes, muffed tackles and the like) are entirely the result of our feeding garbled information into our computers. Feed in the right information and those kicks will go over, those passes will be held and those tackles completed.

Now, so that we get nice and comfortable with our in-built computer, let's give it a name. Let's call it Siggy. We've given it this name as an acknowledgement of the work of probably the most famous shrink of all time, Sigmund Freud (1856–1939), the father of psychoanalysis. Though remembered as much for his wacky ideas —he had some pretty far-out ones relating to sex and dreaming— as for his smart ones, Freud probably taught us more about the mechanics of the human mind than anyone. He may not have got everything right, but he sure improved our understanding of the way our minds work. You could even go so far as to say that he opened the door for electronics engineers to begin developing computers modelled on the human mind.

So, meet Siggy, our personal in-built computer. And Siggy, meet our rugby player, the reader.

Siggy's a clever bloke, a walking brain box. Not only that, but he's the most honest and straight-up character you'll ever meet. He can't lie, and he takes on board every single thing you say to him. On top of all this, he just happens to think so much of you that he'll do just about anything you ask of him, no matter how difficult or complex—or even stupid. Siggy's the kind of bloke who'll perform the impossible for you. All you've got to do is provide him with a stream of pure and uncluttered information. Just as Freud taught us how the human mind works, so Siggy operates as the brain's machinery, its nuts and bolts, its internal combustion engine—your personal in-built supercomputer.

Practising awareness

When you first took up rugby, you concentrated on acquiring that most basic of skills, catching (pass-receiving). No doubt the coach drummed into you the importance of keeping your eye on the ball. You were to watch the ball throughout its trajectory and not take your eyes off it until it was safely in your hands. Since moving the ball through successive pairs of hands is the main means of eluding the opposition and getting it over their goal line, you can't afford to drop it. Just about the worst sound a player can hear in a rugby match is the groan of the spectators—and the hoots of the opposition's supporters—when a simple catch is dropped with the line open. The simpler the catch, the bigger the groan/hoot. In rugby the simplest errors take on far greater meaning than just their immediate effect: the dropped catch might mean a missed try, but more importantly it's a hint that the attacking team is rattled. Hence the coach pleading with you to keep your eye on the ball.

But what is the coach really asking you to do? He's asking you to practise awareness, to understand that Siggy operates exactly like a man-made computer, and if there's not enough accurate data coming in, Siggy can't deliver the results you want.

Let's look more closely at the data Siggy needs to collect that simple pass safely. Siggy's already organising an immensely complex set of muscles and bones and sinews (you) travelling in one direction at anything up to 500 metres a minute (30 kilometres an hour). He then has to assess the flight-path of this oval object (the ball) travelling in a lateral direction at twice that speed, work out the point of interception between the oval object and you, and arrange your hands and arms to receive it.

That's a huge amount of information required for the simple act of catching a ball on the run. Siggy makes these immensely complex calculations in a fraction of a second, and the only means he has of absorbing all the complex information involved is your senses, especially your eyes. If you start to feed in other unnecessary information—such as the position of an approaching tackler—before Siggy has had time to work out the catching equation, you're going to drop that simple catch.

That's why coaches harp on about keeping your eyes on the ball. What they're saying is that the more accurate and concise the information your eyes feed into Siggy, the more sure you can be that Siggy's calculations will be right, and that you'll catch the ball.

Similarly with tackling: most tackles are missed not because the tackler doesn't have a good technique, nor because the ball-carrier is especially strong or elusive, but because Siggy is being fed either not enough data or a heap of irrelevant data. For example, as well as the important things like the ball-carrier's speed and direction in relation to your own field position, you might inadvertently pump into Siggy information about the oncoming player's size and the look on his face. Neither of these bits of information is of any value to Siggy in setting you up to make the tackle. They're a distraction. They distort the important data that Siggy really needs.

If you tell Siggy that the ball-carrier is a huge chap with a ferocious look on his face, Siggy will assume you want these facts taken into account in positioning yourself for the tackle. In processing this extra information, Siggy might, for example, change your body's point of aim from the ball-carrier's knees to his shoulders, because Siggy might guess your priority is really to minimise the risk of getting hurt in the impact. Accordingly, Siggy organises you to aim high so that the only part of you that makes contact with the ball-carrier is your arms. Result? Siggy greatly increases the chances of the tackler shrugging you off, or of you being penalised for a high tackle.

Siggy delivers performance on the basis of all of the information he's fed. Siggy has no filtering mechanism. He can't distinguish between good and useful information, and the bad and useless. Siggy uses the lot, regardless. So the onus is on you—Siggy's eyes and ears and other senses—to feed in only the information Siggy needs to tackle the job (or player) in hand. No more, no less.

The lesson we take from this is that awareness is not something that you pull on with your footy jersey. It's not just a matter of absorbing information—it's a matter of absorbing useful information while at the same time excluding the useless. And that takes practice.

Anyone who has played around on computers knows that there are two basic types of information: the stuff we store long term, and the stuff we need only in the short term. Long-term information is stored on the computer's hard disk, which is a sort of play-back memory capacity built right into the computer's superstructure. Hard disk information is in the computer for good. It doesn't disappear into cyber-nothing when you switch the computer off. It stays in the computer like bullets in the magazine of a gun, to be loaded into the breech when short-term information arrives saying that there's a target in sight.

The other type of information a computer needs is short-term data. The operator feeds this into the computer, which absorbs and processes it on its Random Access Memory (RAM). The computer retains this information only in the short term, and it's usually wiped out when the computer is switched off.

Imagine the computer as a simple calculator, and that you want to find out what you get from multiplying, say, five by ten. The hard disk is the part of the computer that contains the capacity to do the multiplication exercise. It stays in the computer permanently. The figures you want to multiply, the five and the ten, are fed into the computer's short-term memory, the RAM, by the operator. The computer's job is to run the figures the operator has given it through its hard disk to come up with the answer.

The basic techniques of rugby, such as catching or tackling, are stored inside your in-built computer, Siggy, in exactly the same way that permanent data is stored on a computer's hard disk. You store your basic rugby techniques there during practice. The more you practise, the greater the detail you store. The greater the detail you store, the more situations Siggy can respond to usefully when you feed in the short-term data you observe on the playing field.

As with hard disk information on a computer, the more (relevant) short-term data you cram into Siggy, the more effective the performance Siggy delivers. It's this act of gathering up information that we call awareness.

In the match situation, Siggy takes as little as a millisecond to recover the appropriate package of data from his hard disk, then uses it to process the information being fed in through your senses (your RAM) to produce the outcome you desire—the execution of the particular catch or tackle.

Let's see how this works in practice, taking the skill that Grant Fox was perhaps most famous for, his goal-kicking. The hours Fox spent practising goal-kicking by himself stocked up the hard disk of his computer, his Siggy, with a huge base of permanent, relevant information to refer to while playing. Come game-time, Fox simply dug out the goal-kicking information he had stored on his hard disk, matched it with the short-term information he gathered as he lined up the penalty or conversion, and proceeded to kick the goal.

The hard disk information is the basic technique, installed and refined by practice, and the RAM data is the variables—distance, direction, wind, playing surface—that change with circumstance.

Now there's an important thing to note here, which will become a theme throughout this book. It's this: in absorbing and passing on short-term information for, say, a kick, the kicker must *never* include his assessments or opinions about either the difficulty or the importance of what he is about to attempt.

It was one of Grant Fox's great strengths as a kicker that it made no difference whether he was lining up a conversion from in front of the posts that would put Auckland or the All Blacks 30 points ahead of the opposition instead of just 28, or whether it was an angled penalty from way out when his team was a point behind with time up in a crucial match. Fox gave equal importance to every attempted goal. He went through precisely the same routine for every goal kick, whether it was important to the outcome of the match or not. Remember that routine of his? The hand-shaking, the long looks from the ball to the goalposts and back?

The lesson Fox teaches us from this is that it's meaningless to Siggy whether the kick is a hard one or an easy one, whether it's important in the context of the game or not. Questions of a kick's difficulty or importance are counterproductive to Siggy. They simply confuse him. All Siggy wants to do is kick the damn thing. He doesn't want to be distracted by having to evaluate the task on scales of difficulty or importance.

The thing about Siggy is that he will make use of every bit of data you feed him, whether it's useful or not. The only data Siggy needs is the accurate, factual information required for him to perform the task at hand.

Your eyes and your other senses are Siggy's keyboard, and you need to use them not only to ensure all the relevant information registers with Siggy, but also to ensure you exclude irrelevant and judgemental information.

It's important, then, that you don't put a bias (what politicians — and halfbacks—call a 'spin') on the information you pass on to Siggy. It's meaningless to Siggy that you think the ball is approaching at a speed or height that could make it difficult to catch, or that the ball-carrier is an ugly brute with thighs like fenceposts. Siggy just wants the facts: the ball, or the ball-carrier, is travelling in such-and-such a direction at such-and-such a speed. All you have to do is keep your eyes on the ball or the ball-carrier, let them do the talking to Siggy, and leave it to Siggy to make the necessary calculations and adjustments.

The information you feed Siggy has to be cold and clinical. It's the only kind of information he can handle. Anything else will confuse him.

To understand how effective Siggy can be in processing information and using it to deal with specific situations, watch a baby learning to walk. Walking involves an extraordinarily complex series of muscle contractions, programmed by signals sent to and from the brain to all parts of the body. It's information that none of us is born with—we all have to learn it. The baby's personal in-built computer is undeveloped: it comes with very little data stored in it, but what it has got is not yet cluttered up with negatives like fear of failure, and self-doubt.

In learning to walk, the baby makes mistakes like falling on its backside, but each time it does so it's supplying its brain with new information. Siggy keeps making the necessary corrections on the basis of the steady in-flow of factual data provided by the senses until, finally, the baby can walk upright and set about wrecking the house and driving its parents up the wall just the way nature intended it to.

The baby doesn't make value judgements about all the times it fell over while learning to walk. The baby doesn't swear or throw up its arms in disgust or even get mad: it's too busy absorbing information, practising awareness, to resort to silly histrionics that do nothing but distort the information-feeding process. The baby is simply aware of its mistakes and automatically trusts Siggy to learn from them. And Siggy delivers.

To a baby, a mistake is neither good nor bad. It's just part of the information-gathering process and, as such, mistakes are just as useful as successes. Humans learn more in their first seven years than at any other stage in their lives. They learn quickly because no one has taught them to interfere with their brain functions by offering opinion or judgement. Babies are simply aware of what they want to achieve, and they allow Siggy to learn the skills involved without interference.

The process of learning to walk is vastly more complex than the process of learning to catch a football or tackle a ball-carrier. A baby can absorb and process so much information in so short a time because it doesn't start out with its mental processes confused by judgements, fear of failure and self-doubt. Sadly, it will pick up these things later in life to a greater or lesser degree, and it will never again be able to learn so much so quickly. By the time the child gets to school, its learning capacity will already be approaching a decline that will probably continue throughout its life—unless it makes a conscious effort (as you are doing now) to arrest that decline by rediscovering the learning process that came to it naturally as a baby.

By contrast, a lifetime of value judgements puts huge obstacles in the way of an adult learning something new. It should be a lot easier, for example, for an adult to learn to ride a horse than for a baby to learn to walk, but any riding instructor will tell you it's harder teaching an adult than a child. Instructors may politely explain this by saying adults aren't as 'supple' as children, but what they mean is that adults' natural instinct and flair for learning has become warped over the years by their becoming judgemental.

Note that it's the *ability* to learn that's become warped, not the *capacity* to learn. Remembering the pain of having fallen over at ground level, adults become alarmed at the prospect of falling from way up there on the back of a horse. So they bombard Siggy with this judgemental information, this fear, and Siggy responds by having them hang on for all they're worth—they tense their muscles, grit their teeth, clench the reins like a lifeline, and otherwise do everything they can to let the horse know they've no right to be on its back. The horse often responds by making the very thing happen that the adult learner-rider feared in the first place. So if you want to learn to ride without being repeatedly dumped on your backside, you need to know how *not* to mess Siggy up with irrelevant judgements which simply amount to fear of failure.

Accumulating accurate data

We've now seen that, as rugby players, our most important function is to provide Siggy with data—just bare facts—with no judgements or interpretations attached. And you've no doubt realised that, unless this data is as accurate as you can get it, Siggy won't be able to respond by giving your muscles the precise set of instructions needed to deal with the situation at hand.

Years of watching and playing rugby will teach you that if only you knew the whereabouts of every player on the field at any given time, you'd be in the best possible position to work out how to turn any given situation to your team's advantage. As a player, you know where everybody's supposed to be in relation to the ball but, because rugby is a highly fluid and mobile game, about the only times any player is where he ought to be is at kick-offs and set pieces. The rest of the time, everybody is scrambling to get back or forward to the position they're supposed to be in, relative to the ball, and every metre that the ball travels in any direction changes what those positions should be anyway. This means that the most important information your eyes could possibly feed Siggy in any given split second would be the field-position of every single player in relation to the ball. This what you aim at.

Accumulating and updating all that data both accurately and constantly is mentally possible, because the average human brain has more than enough short-term memory for the job. But it's physically impossible to do it while you're actually playing, because you're often in a heap on the ground and can't see more than a metre around you, or your vision is obscured by other players. Also, unless you recognise each of the opposing players, you won't know what positions they play without seeing their numbers. There are also all those times when circumstances set you a particular task—kicking or passing or receiving or tackling—and you've got to concentrate on doing that to the exclusion of anything else that's going on around you. So keeping Siggy informed of the field-position of every single player in relation to the ball is not possible all of the time. But it's vital most of the time.

The process goes like this: you absorb information all the time you're off the ball—which is most of the time for the outer backs, and a lot of the time even for the most involved players, like loose forwards. You train your mind to update constantly the accurate, nonjudgemental information you feed Siggy. And it's a job well within everyone's mental capacity.

Awareness of the ball and of the other players' relation to it was, of course, the peculiar genius of Grant Fox. He usually had a better idea than any other player on the field of where everyone ought to be, and of when they weren't there. As a fly half in charge of tactical decision-making, Fox knew instantly if, for example, the opposing fullback was far enough out of position for the deep kick to be the most productive option at that given moment. The wisdom of Fox's option-taking is legendary. He was heart-breaking to play against because he always seemed to know which option, out of the range available to him, would do the most damage. And the reason Fox was so good at choosing the right option was because he deliberately and constantly practised awareness of, and accumulated accurate data about, where everyone was in relation to the ball.

The only way to develop the skill of accurately telling Siggy where the ball and all the players are on the field is to practise being aware. You can do this at any time, on or off the rugby field. Wherever you are, every now and then throw a quick glance about you, then close your eyes and try to locate in your mind's eye as many of the people or objects that you saw. Or, to test your awareness, spend ten seconds looking at the page of a newspaper, then close your eyes and see how many headlines you can remember. Not many, eh? Yet, if you practised doing this you would soon be able to rattle off every headline.

Exercises like this are aimed first at making you realise how shallow your powers of observation are—how little data your eyes usually absorb—and then at making you realise the huge capacity your brain has for absorbing and processing data once it has been trained.

Throughout this book you'll find more tips and practical advice to help you programme Siggy, your personal in-built computer, to make a better rugby player of you. But first, we need a deeper understanding of our own human nature and how it makes it hard for us to supply Siggy with the only thing he needs and can use: pure, uncluttered facts.

–2–
Meet Napoleon, the temperamental emperor

> Without this playing with fantasy, no creative work has ever yet come to birth. The debt we owe to the play of imagination is incalculable. CARL JUNG

At the beginning of this book we guaranteed to improve your game regardless of your age, sex, natural ability or the level at which you're presently playing. This was not a promise made lightly. The secret of improvement, however, doesn't lie solely in greater fitness or skill, though Grant Fox will give some advice in both these areas later in this book.

The reason this book can guarantee improvement is that, in its overall approach to rugby, it recognises the paramount importance of attitude, and that an attitude that is conducive to better rugby is made, not born. Attitude, more than any other factor, makes the difference between success and failure, in rugby as in life.

In the first half of this century, people relied almost exclusively on developing their physical skills and fitness as the main means of improving their sporting performance. After World War II, however, it became increasingly apparent—especially to the Eastern bloc countries like the Soviet Union and East Germany—that the purely physical capacity to improve performance had, to a large degree, reached its limit. To get an edge over the West in the sporting sphere—one of the few areas in which it consistently held an advantage during the Cold War—the Eastern bloc began to put just about as much emphasis on the mental aspects of sporting competition as on the physical.

As a result, Communist countries rapidly began to dominate world sport, especially at that pinnacle of international competition, the Olympic Games. Western countries, although initially slow to adapt to this change because of a lingering affection for amateurism, eventually began to follow the lead provided by the Communists, setting up programmes to explore the previously ignored realms of attitude-related performance.

These days sports psychologists are beginning to be regarded as almost as important to improved performance as coaches, but, generally speaking, the West has been slow on the uptake.

The rugby codes have been no faster than other sports in picking up on these changes. As a result, performance has been largely related to a combination of natural ability and developed physical skills and fitness.

Since the start of the professional era in rugby union, a profound change has taken place in both rugby codes, with mental preparation at last being accorded its rightful prominence at all levels of the game, and with most international and professional sides these days employing the services of a sports psychologist—the team shrink. Also, right back at the grass roots of the game, schoolchildren are being introduced early on to the notion of improvement in the game through the training of the mind as well as the body.

In New Zealand, in the late 1970s, a lot of cynicism greeted the emergence of mental conditioning as a feature of rugby preparation. It would be fair to say that no single player in the New Zealand game did more than Grant Fox to break down these prejudices. At a time when soccer-style round-the-corner goal-kicking with the instep was replacing the head-on torpedo and upright styles of toe-kicking, Fox burst into prominence with his slow and methodical addressing of the ball—to exactly the same pattern each time. In his early days of playing for Auckland, he took some awful flak from opposing spectators for his careful and deliberate preparation, but he gradually wore this resistance down by the only method no one could argue with: more of his goal attempts went over than anyone else's. Today, the great New Zealand kickers of the oval ball—from Andrew Mehrtens and Matthew Cooper in union, to Darryl Halligan and Matthew Ridge in league—use the same deliberate approach.

In his field-play no less than in his goal-kicking, Grant Fox introduced to New Zealand rugby the notion that mental preparation is just as important as physical preparation. From there he was able to demonstrate that there are essentially two elements to every person's mental make-up. You have already been introduced to one of these: Siggy, our personal in-built computer who responds —in exactly the same way that an electronic computer does—to electrical impulses sent to him from all over your body.

Siggy has no emotion. He responds simply and innocently to the messages he gets—all of them. If the stomach sends him a message saying 'I am empty' and the eyes send another message saying 'Food is available', Siggy responds by directing the muscles to convey the food to the mouth, and the eating process begins. Siggy doesn't have any feelings about this process one way or the other. He just does it. Siggy is a mechanical device.

Siggy's capacity for receiving and transmitting signals seems to be almost infinite. Scientists believe the average human employs only about a tenth of the brain's capacity, so the potential for improvement is obvious: all we have to do is improve the quality of the information we feed Siggy.

What makes humans different from animals and plants is that we can choose the kinds of messages we send to the brain, and the sort of package we send them in. That's because humans are endowed with a second unique and wonderful gift, apart from the computer we call Siggy. This gift is our imagination, and it has evolved in an extraordinary way.

Back in the days when we all lived in caves, the evolving humanoid developed what is today called the 'fight or flight' syndrome. This was a choice of what to do when faced with danger: we could stay and meet it head-on (fight), or we could run for our dear lives (flight). Whichever decision we made, Siggy—yes, he was already around by then—responded accordingly.

But the important thing is this: we had a choice. And the only reason we had a choice was because we had an imagination. You can't have choice without one. If you cannot imagine the likely outcome of one chosen action over another, you don't have choice. Imagination and choice go hand in hand.

With an imagination that could look into the future and predict the likely outcomes of the various responses available to us, we were able to decide in a split second what course of action to take. Siggy could then be activated, and hormones such as adrenalin released so that we dealt with the situation to the best of our ability.

Environmental conditioning has seen this gift evolve to such a degree that humans now recognise danger even when it doesn't exist. This is, if you like, the downside of having choice, of having imagination.

The worst manifestations of an overactive imagination can be seen in phobias like arachnophobia (fear of spiders), agoraphobia (fear of open spaces) and claustrophobia (fear of confined spaces). When the arachnophobic sees a harmless little spider, their imagination kicks in and perceives a danger even though there isn't one. Siggy responds to the message, adrenalin starts flowing, the heart rate increases, body temperature rises, muscles tense—and the phobic screams and flees. Sure, the fear is irrational, but that doesn't make it any less real to the phobic.

A different manifestation of imagination is when someone delivers some sort of superhuman performance (the upside of imagination). The classic case is of the frail little lady who suddenly finds the strength to lift up a car to free a loved one trapped underneath. There are countless documented examples of such absolutely unbelievable feats performed by the most unlikely people.

What happens in such cases is that the messages sent to Siggy identify a desperate danger—a real one this time. In extreme situations the messages coming through to Siggy are so clear, so graphic, so powerful and so rapid that there is no time for them to pick up the usual clutter of doubts and negative thoughts along the way. They even fail to pick up on the common knowledge that frail little ladies can't lift cars. The effect of these utterly pure and uncontaminated signals on Siggy is to trigger a response (in this example, brute strength) far more powerful than the person could have believed possible if they'd had time to think about it.

It's this latent strength, hidden within each and every one of us, that this book will teach you to tap into. We're going to train our minds to send Siggy messages of such clarity and precision—such pure and uncluttered data—that he's able to focus all the body's resources on delivering the most effective possible response to any given situation.

So let's give a name to this extraordinary tool we otherwise know as our imagination. Let's call him Napoleon.

He gets this name from two famous but very different characters, both of whom have relevance to the sort of personality that our own Napoleon comprises. The first is Napoleon Bonaparte and the second is Napoleon Hill. Bonaparte (1769–1821) was a colourful little bloke who combined practical genius—both as a lawmaker and a military strategist—with a crazy romanticism that made him want to conquer the world. He met his Waterloo in 1815, just a few years before William Webb Ellis picked up a football and ran with it at Rugby School.

Napoleon Hill was one of a long line of American writers and motivators who turned Sigmund Freud's new-found understanding of the mechanics of the human mind into what is today the vast self-improvement industry. Hill's best-known book is probably *Keys to Positive Thinking—Ten Steps to Health, Wealth and Success*. It ranks up there with Norman Vincent Peale's *The Power of Positive Thinking* as one of the icons of self-improvement literature.

In giving the name Napoleon to our imagination, we're acknowledging its capacity both for practical brilliance, and for getting carried away with impractical ideas. It's the first half of this two-sided character—the practical brilliance—that we need to tap in the process of selecting and feeding pure and uncluttered information into our personal in-built supercomputer, our Siggy.

So, meet Napoleon, our imaginative information-gatherer. And Napoleon, meet our rugby-player, our reader.

Now, as we've seen from the earlier examples, of both destructive phobias and phenomenal performances, Napoleon has both his upside and his downside. But the first vital thing to recognise about Napoleon is that he's a completely separate entity from Siggy. Napoleon is just as important as Siggy, but the two are as different and as separate as a hammer and a chisel. Sure, they work in tandem, but they're completely different tools.

We also need to see Napoleon and Siggy as separate entities not only in space, but also in time. Napoleon tends to live in either the past (reminiscing about things that were, or might have been) or in the future (imagining things that might yet happen), while Siggy lives exclusively in the present. Siggy is the computer. Napoleon is the operator.

The unfortunate thing about their relationship is that imaginative Napoleon tends to put a spin (a subjective interpretation) on the information he passes to Siggy and Siggy acts instantaneously on *all* the information he gets from Napoleon. Napoleon's spin is based on what has happened in the past, or may happen in the future, and doesn't give Siggy credit for the limitless potential he has to achieve things in the present.

The classic example of this in sport was the breaking of the four-minute mile. Early in the twentieth century the so-called experts reckoned it was impossible to run a mile (1609 metres) in 240 seconds. And for years athletes believed them. Any number of famous runners hammered away at this magical mark, only to finish a few seconds outside it. Then, just when the runners were about convinced that the experts were right, an English doctor named Roger Bannister stepped out one fine day in 1954 and, by more than half a second, proved that the impossible was possible after all. And what do you know? That opened the floodgates. Within weeks no fewer than four other runners had duplicated the feat.

Today a man is nothing in international middle-distance running until he has at least a few four-minute miles under his belt—and New Zealand's 1976 Olympic 1500 metres champion, John Walker, had actually clocked up a hundred of them by the time he retired. In fact, Walker built on Bannister's achievement by pulling off another 'impossibility': the first mile run under 3 minutes 50 seconds, at Goteborg, Sweden, in 1975. Today the top male international middle-distance runners are knocking on the door of 3 minutes 40 seconds. So how impossible is 'impossible'?

The achievement of Roger Bannister, who started it all, is probably the single most famous example in sport of mind triumphing over matter, and the lesson for us is that when Napoleon makes decisions on the basis of history alone, he's failing to recognise his partner Siggy's limitless potential to rewrite it.

When somebody else comes along and rewrites history, Napoleon is forced to accept it was possible after all, and suddenly the seemingly impossible becomes achievable—as it did for the four runners who so quickly emulated Bannister's feat. By then, of course, it was Bannister's name that was writ large on the pages of history. Hardly anyone remembers or cares who the other four were.

Napoleon and Siggy work exactly the same way when asked to face the multiple challenges of rugby football. The quality of a rugby player's performance can't be measured the way a runner's can: a four-minute mile is undeniable evidence of running quality, but no such empirical standards exist in rugby.

Quality in a rugby performance exists in only two places: in the eye of the observer (the spectator, the team-mate, the opponent, the coach, the selector) and in the mind of the player. We, as players, have little or no control over what observers think is a quality rugby performance, but we are in complete control of our own powers of quality judgement. At the end of the day it doesn't really matter how anyone else thinks we played. Only we, the players, really know whether we've played badly or well, because we're the only ones who can read our minds.

This is a central point to the ideas you will encounter in this book, so let's repeat it: it doesn't matter a damn what anyone else thinks of the way you play rugby. All that matters is the way you feel about your game. If you think you played badly, you're right. If you think you played well, you're right. It doesn't matter what anyone else thinks.

'But what about the selectors?' you might ask. 'If they think I played badly, they won't select me, whether I thought I played well or not. And, after all, it's the selectors who decide whether I continue at this level of the game or move on up to the next one.'

This is true. But can you get into the selector's mind to see what he's really after in a player? Obviously not. There is only one single mind you can get into, and that's your own. Yours is the only mind that you have to satisfy, and if you come off the pitch at the end of the game convinced you played right up to your potential, then that's the highest satisfaction you can aspire to. The selector or coach, sports writer or mentor can and does set broad goals and performance parameters for you to aim at, but it's ultimately up to you—and you alone—to decide whether or not you've reached them.

Getting selected for higher honours is always, to some degree, a matter of luck. We can all cite cases of someone we reckon should have been chosen for, say, a national team, but missed out. Like it or not, your advancement in the game is dependent to some degree on the vagaries of selection, and if you don't like the judgement that one selector makes of your performance, you are free to move to another club, competition or country where the selectors' ideals of quality play are closer to your own. But there's no point in trying to be all things to all selectors: in the end, if they don't select you they don't select you, and that's all there is to it. And in that event there is only one comfort: the certain knowledge that your performance was consistently the best you could deliver.

In summary, you can't rely on anyone else's judgement of your ability because that judgement will change with the person making it. The only judgement over which you have control is your own—so that's the only one that counts in the long run.

The importance of this attitude will become clearer as we tackle subjects like goal-setting, but for now it's enough to realise that ultimately the only opinion that counts is your own. If you want to perform to your optimum, you cannot afford to have your Napoleon trying to put a selector's spin on the information he's feeding to Siggy.

Napoleon's job is to practise awareness—that sponge-like absorption of information—so he can feed as much pure and uncluttered data into Siggy as possible. The problem with Napoleon is that, being imaginative, he has this huge tendency to put an imaginative spin on the data he's transmitting to Siggy. Lining up for a critical, try-saving tackle, Napoleon finds himself remembering how he fouled up the last time he was in this situation (living in the past), or imagining the ribbing he'll get from his team-mates after the game if he misses this tackle (living in the future). Consequently, Napoleon delivers to Siggy all the classic fight-or-flight signals instead of the clear and uncluttered information Siggy needs to organise the tackle. And Siggy reacts accordingly.

His task may be simple—all he has to do is organise the body to tackle the ball-carrier—but Napoleon is complicating it by sending a whole lot of irrelevant information along with the relevant stuff like the ball-carrier's speed and direction. This makes Siggy's job vastly more difficult: instead of just having to organise the body to make the tackle, Siggy is also being asked by Napoleon to (a) not repeat the cock-up of a tackle he performed last time he was in this situation, and (b) not do anything to attract ridicule from his teammates when the match is over. That's far too much for Siggy to sort out and prioritise in the split second he has available to line up the tackle. So in the confusion he botches it. It's not Siggy's fault: all he did was to receive and try to act on *all* the messages Napoleon sent him.

What Napoleon should have done was to exclude his fears about both the past and the future from the messages he sent Siggy. Napoleon needs to learn to operate strictly in the present. Napoleon must learn to deliver messages that contain no elements of fear or self-doubt, no reference to the past or the future.

In short, Napoleon must learn to concentrate on absorbing relevant information (i.e. practising awareness) and passing it on to Siggy without any negative spin attached. We call this practice 'concentration'. And, as we'll see in the next chapter, concentration is an art.

−3−
The art of concentration

> Put all your eggs in one basket, and WATCH THAT BASKET! **Mark Twain**

People who marvel at a top sportsperson for being relaxed or 'cool' are talking about a Siggy-orientated competitor. Everyone remembers the icy temperament and stony-faced composure of the great Swedish tennis player Bjorn 'Ice' Borg as he notched up Wimbledon triumphs year after year; the coolly relaxed demeanour of Tiger Woods as he holed a multi-metre putt to win a golf classic; and the breathless ease with which Grant Fox potted a goal from a tricky angle to convert yet another All Black try.

You could say that these are all naturally gifted sportspeople, and that it was their natural gifts—their raw talent—that allowed them to become leaders in their fields. But that's to believe that temperament is born, not made. Oh sure, there's no denying some people have more natural sporting ability and better natural temperament than others but, by the same token, everyone is gifted to some extent, and today nobody gets to the top of any major sport on natural ability alone. Whatever our quota of natural talent, and however much we enhance it by physical practice and conditioning, we can realise our full potential only if we take on board one fundamental reality—what you might call the basic sports equation:

Performance = your natural and acquired Siggy potential, minus the level of negative interference from Napoleon

To realise your performance potential you've got to develop faith in your particular natural and acquired ability—in other words you've got to grow in self-confidence. You do that by feeding ever more pure and uncluttered data into Siggy. At the same time you reduce or divert the amount of irrelevant material generated by Napoleon—that little voice in your head constantly trying to put a bias on the information passed on to Siggy.

The people who benefit most from the principles and techniques outlined in this book are those who admit to varying degrees of self-doubt—which should be just about everyone. Above all, this book helps the 'chokers', the people whose temperament (or nerve) lets them down at crucial times and prevents them from playing as well as they could.

You know the feeling: the tight, nauseous knot in the gut as you approach the match that determines in your own mind whether you've made a significant advance in the sport, or whether you're doomed to be just another plodder making up the team numbers. For many sportspeople—some famous champions included—the feelings are so strong they vomit before a match.

All of these reactions are symptoms of the old caveman fight-or-flight syndrome, which is still with us to this day, buried deep in our genes. The syndrome is triggered when Napoleon perceives himself to be in a dangerous situation—the danger of making a fool of himself. 'How will I be able to hold my head up if I fumble a pass or miss a tackle?' he asks himself. 'What if I play badly? What if my marker shows me up by playing brilliantly? Won't this make all the training and practice I've put in a complete waste of time?'

The usual reaction of the victim of these feelings ('the butterflies', 'the screaming willies'—call them what you like) is to vow and declare to try harder, to concentrate. And that's the great mistake. The fact is that trying harder is usually fatal for Siggy. If you have to try to concentrate, you're not concentrating.

Instead of responding to your nerves just by trying to concentrate on playing well, step back a little and give some thought to what's actually going on inside you. Napoleon (it's all his fault!) has convinced you that there's a danger ahead—but that's just plain nonsense. What danger? Is the world going to fall apart if you drop a catch, fluff a kick or fail to show up for a ruck? Are your team-mates going to stage a public lynching in the middle of the pitch if your line-out throws are a bit off-target? Is your making a few mistakes going to trigger a war in a distant continent? Come on, Napoleon, get real; get a life! Whether it be a pre-season friendly or a World Cup final, the world's going to go on its merry way whether you play well or badly. The sun will rise again tomorrow. Life will go on.

Thinking this way is the first step towards taking control of those powerful feelings. It puts them in perspective, in their true place within your world and the wider world. It gives you that breathing space you need to realise that all that's happening to you is that silly old Napoleon has perceived an urgent danger when there isn't one; silly old Napoleon is turning loose all those caveman flight-or-fight chemicals inside you.

In doing so, Napoleon is pretty well guaranteeing you'll lose. He is also unwittingly defeating the purpose of your taking up the game in the first place, which is to enjoy yourself. What's the point in playing a game—any game—that renders you sick with the fear of losing? What's the point in stepping out for a game, especially an important one, if all you wish is that it was over before it started, or that you knew the outcome in advance so all you had to do was come to terms with it? Where's the enjoyment in that?

You are supposed to be playing this game for the fun of it, for the appreciation of the competition, the challenge, and the shared joy of being part of a team that strives together and may even happen to win a game or several. There should be no place for feeling as if a volcano is erupting in your stomach—at least not unless that's a sign that you're going to play brilliantly.

The extreme 'choker', the person who is completely victimised by these feelings, may even be in the grip of a phobia, suffering the same overwhelming reaction as the arachnophobic who sees a spider. In most cases the 'choker' syndrome can be overcome, first by understanding the mechanics of it, then by attacking it with a mind-training programme aimed at turning the choking liability into a winning asset. The sportsperson with a bad case of 'the butterflies' is simply undergoing a natural, though exaggerated, reaction with potentially enormous benefits to their performance—*if they can harness that potential.*

Changing that internal chemical reaction from a liability into an asset to your game is simply a matter of technique, of mind-training. And you've already taken the first step in acquiring that technique by putting those irrational fears into a rational perspective. The next step is to make those irrational fears work for you, instead of against you.

So what should be going through your mind as you approach a match? Your only concern should be to feed Siggy pure and uncluttered data, while ignoring Napoleon and his fight-or-flight syndrome, his negative futurising, his wallowing in an unhappy past. Your real need is to play in the now. Napoleon's job is just to feed the relevant data into Siggy without putting a subjective flight-or-fight spin on it.

Rugby is a stop-start affair—anything up to a minute or two of intense activity followed by a brief hiatus while the players catch up with the action or reassemble for set-play resumptions. Whatever the position you play, your game is a succession of intense and often brief involvements followed by short breaks. This pattern dictates the way you employ Siggy and Napoleon. Generally speaking it goes like this: in the breaks when you're not directly involved in play, you engage Napoleon full-on practising awareness, absorbing pure and uncluttered information (without letting Napoleon put his negative spin on it); then, during the periods when you're directly involved in the play, you switch Napoleon off entirely and let Siggy run on autopilot, fuelled by Napoleon's pure and uncluttered data.

This on-off rhythm varies with each of the fifteen playing positions. Generally speaking, the forwards have longer periods of direct involvement, and shorter breaks in between, while the backs have it the other way round. Each position makes unique demands on the player: the scrum half and the fly half usually have less time out between engagements than the wings and the fullback, just as the loose forwards tend to be more constantly engaged than the tight forwards.

So let's see how it works in practice. The individual player encounters two sorts of stops in the course of the game:

1. The spell following a breakdown when the teams organise themselves into set-plays for scrums, line-outs, penalties, free kicks and kickoffs.

2. The travelling downtime when play has left the player behind and he's running to catch up.

You turn Napoleon full-on during these stop periods so he can bring Siggy up to speed with the latest developments in the game. These stop periods are Napoleon-time, and there are three types of information that Napoleon needs to feed Siggy during them:

1. Where you are. The first thing Siggy needs to know is your position on the pitch—in relation to the ball, in relation to your team-mates, and in relation to your playing position.
2. Where you ought to be. The second thing Siggy needs to know is where you ought to be in relation to where the ball's going, in relation to where your team-mates are heading or reassembling, and in relation to your playing position.
3. What you need to do when you arrive where you ought to be. Siggy needs to be told how the game is going to resume (scrum, line-out, kick) and his role in the resumption.

Once Napoleon has passed on all this data, just turn him off and cut him out of the process. Napoleon has no further role until the next break in play. Once Siggy has been given all the information, leave it up to him to decide how to apply it. In the hours of practice leading up to the game, you've stocked Siggy's hard disk up with all the information he needs to hit that ruck (the body position, the forward momentum, the binding with other players, the pumping of the legs), collect that pass (the eye on the ball, the hands extended to receive), stand in that tackle (the turning back to protect the ball from the opposition, the rolling of the shoulders to deflect back-up tacklers, the looking out for the best-positioned on-coming team-mate to hand the ball off to).

Cut Napoleon out of the loop between stops, and allow Siggy to execute the particular task or sequence of tasks for which his hard disk has been stocked up during practice sessions. Then, when play pauses, reactivate Napoleon immediately as an awareness machine, gobbling up new information on where you are, where you ought to be, and what to do when you get there.

Never—but never—titillate Napoleon with worries about whether Siggy's got the right information on his hard disk to deal with the upcoming tasks. If Siggy hasn't got the precise response stashed away, he'll improvise, often in brilliant and unexpected ways. Siggy is a superb improviser: he can draw on half a dozen or more stored skill files at once to meet any situation, if you just give him his head. Of course the more skill files you store on Siggy's hard disk through practice and experience, the better he'll handle any given situation. Specific skill files needed for each of the positions in a rugby team are covered in Chapter 14.

By doing all of this you give yourself the best possible chance of performing to your potential and, incidentally, you give the disconcerting appearance to your opponents of being relaxed and self-confident. Whatever the outcome, you enjoy yourself because you love the game and love to compete. Decide beforehand that if you lose the game it will be because your opponents played better than you did—and you can live with that. There is never any element of emotional danger in the situation—it's a game of rugby, for crying out loud!—and, whatever Napoleon says, your job is to trust Siggy to produce your best for you.

With these attitudes in place, you can welcome the pre-game butterflies-in-the-stomach feeling as the signal from Napoleon to Siggy that your desire to win is at the right level—and then you can ease back and enjoy the game.

Shortly we'll take a look at how your composure affects your opponents, but first let's develop a formula for switching Napoleon and Siggy on and off successively in tune with the stop-start nature of the game. The switch from Napoleon to Siggy needs to be automatic so it happens without you having to think about it. You develop this capacity through a combination of visualisation (a skill we'll look at later in this book) and repetition. The repetition requires conscious commitment during four successive weekly games in which you focus on switching backwards and forwards from Napoleon to Siggy at the appropriate times. And you need to do it at least 30 times, or constantly throughout the first quarter of each match at least.

Start at the kickoff. As you line up, actively review in your head your kickoff drills—be they for receiving or for kicking off—right up to the moment when the kicker's foot strikes the ball. Then switch Napoleon off, clear your mind of all thought and emotion, and leave it to Siggy to do his stuff. At the first break (usually a line-out) while you're running up to take your position for the restart, run those three core questions through your head:

1. Where am I?
2. Where do I need to go?
3. What do I do when I get there?

Then, the moment the hooker throws the ball in, switch Napoleon off and turn everything over to Siggy.

Do this about 30 times in weekly matches over four weeks and you'll find you're doing it automatically most of the time. This is good, because it means Napoleon is being progressively cut out of the loop for the duration of the match. Pretty soon you'll be going through the whole match on Siggy's autopilot with no interference from Napoleon. If you find emotional old Napoleon creeping back into your game with his worrying and his self-doubt, resort to this exercise and he'll pretty soon shut up.

With this exercise there is one big 'don't': *Don't* let Napoleon start reviewing the previous phase of play at any stage during the game. He mustn't be allowed to tell you you made a lousy—or a great—job of that pass or tackle or ruck. He mustn't be allowed to make any judgements at all on the way you've played while you're still playing. There'll be time enough to review your performance after the match. Napoleon's sole job during the match is to practise awareness, to feed pure and uncluttered information to Siggy.

Follow this formula, perform this exercise, and how do you end up? You end up one cool customer—relaxed, aware, laid-back. 'Cool' is speed without haste, determination without tension.

And this introduces another factor: how are your opponents affected by your composure? The fact is that nothing is more unsettling to a team than an opposing one that keeps its cool no matter what the state of the game or the scoreline. Of course the state of mind of the fourteen other players in your team is not your responsibility (that's a job for the coach or the team shrink). But you can have a big influence—not only a negative one on the opposition but a positive one on your team-mates—if you are the one who keeps his cool while everyone else is losing theirs. When a player remains cool and confident even when his side is getting a hiding the opposition becomes wary—and wariness undermines their concentration and confidence. Their Napoleons begin to say to them, 'Look at this guy: I can't believe how relaxed he is. He must be so confident of winning. What sort of tricks has he got up his sleeve?'

If your opponents allow these feelings to creep into their minds, they are no longer concentrating properly. Then if they make a mistake—of which there is now a stronger likelihood—they'll worry about it. Their concentration will slip. They'll vow to try harder, with the inevitable result that they make even more mistakes. Your 'cool', especially under pressure from the scoreboard, can go a long way to turning a losing match around. Your 'cool'—which people sometimes also refer to as leadership—can inspire your team and dismay the opposition. 'Cool' is effortless concentration.

None of this is to say that taking charge of your Napoleon is a simple thing, or something you can do immediately: it takes time and training to develop the best temperament for the game, especially if you're a naturally tense or highly strung person. But the techniques we describe here will put you on the right path. Use them, practise them, and we guarantee you'll get results.

The better the results the more confidence you'll develop in Siggy, your in-built personal computer that contains the combination of your natural and your learned abilities. The process snowballs, compounding itself like interest in the bank: as your Siggy improves, so does your confidence. And eventually the downside of those attacks of the screaming willies will be a thing of the past, and you'll learn to welcome those pre-match jitters as a barometer of your attitude to the coming match.

–4–
The snowball effect

> If error is corrected whenever it is recognised as such, the path of error is the path of truth. HANS REICHENBACH

Wherever sportspeople meet, one of the most popular topics of conversation is the patch of good or bad form they're going through. It's great when you're on song, with Napoleon feeding pure and uncluttered information into Siggy, and Siggy responding with performances that are skilled, consistent and committed. But then along comes the form slump, and this can be devastating for a player in any sport to come to terms with. It's particularly so in the case of rugby, because you can't solve the problem just by upping the work-rate: form slumps are a product of the mind, not the body, and won't be cured by a few extra miles on the road, hours in the gym or cramming in an extra practice session.

But form slumps can be stopped. And then they can be reversed.

It's how you view the form slump, and then how you go about correcting it, that are critical. Since form slumps are entirely a factor of the mind, the way to tackle them is with more and better mind-training.

First of all, let's define the beast. So-called form slumps are the snowball effect of a decline in confidence. To understand the process, let's go back to our example of the baby learning to walk: no matter how many times it falls over, its imagination isn't developed enough—and the falls don't hurt it badly enough—to slow the learning process. Imagine how difficult it would be for the baby to learn to walk if its Napoleon was fully active, the way an adult's is. After the first fall Napoleon would begin to predict more such painful and humiliating catastrophes and, in trying not to fall over,

Siggy's ability to correct the pattern would be messed up. No doubt the baby would eventually learn to walk, through necessity, but the process would take a lot longer.

In other words, the baby has yet to discover the meaning of confidence, and the significance of lacking it. The baby assumes it'll eventually walk without falling over and, because it assumes that, it's naturally confident. It takes the falling over in its stride—literally. It seldom actually hurts itself—when you're less than a metre tall the ground's not that far away, and your backside is padded with nappies—and it hasn't learnt to feel humiliated when it loses its balance and plonks back down on its bottom. Consequently, the information its Napoleon is feeding to its Siggy is uncluttered by fear of failure.

A human being's fastest rate of learning is in the time immediately following birth, and it declines steadily from then on. A child is born with billions of brain cells, called neurons, of which only a relative few—such as those governing its breathing, its digestive functions and the beating of its heart—come pre-connected. Babies often have to be taught even to suckle.

The process of hooking neurons up to each other (which is itself a definition of learning) is one of experience. Behaviour is formed by cells, driven by experience, reaching out and forming pathways to other cells. The pathways are strengthened each time the experience is repeated.

The pathways can also dissolve through lack of use. One instance of this occurs in Japanese babies who, like all babies, are born with the ability to distinguish between 'r' and 'l' sounds when they hear them. But because there is no 'l' sound in the language they hear their parents speak, Japanese babies quickly forget the distinction and, should they learn to speak English in later life, will tend to pronounce all 'l' sounds as 'r' ones.

By the time a child is two, the neurons in its brain have made at least 300 trillion (that's 300,000,000,000,000) connections, including the ones required for it to walk upright and to communicate in a limited fashion. And it will never again learn so much so fast as long as it lives.

The challenge for the sportsperson is to adapt the baby's learning processes to their own personal goals. This involves building ever more confidence by allowing Siggy to receive ever more pure and uncluttered data from Napoleon. As the rugby player begins to succeed, where once he floundered, his confidence grows and he becomes less likely to make the mistakes that delayed success for him in the first place.

This is the natural and positive progression of the learning cycle. But thanks to our friend Napoleon, who has an ever increasing influence on our learning capacity as we grow older, there can also be the negative progression that brings about a loss of form.

Failure to overcome an obstacle can be either a positive or a negative influence in the learning cycle. A player performing below his potential can either look at why he's doing so, with the aim of improving the aspects of his game that let him down, or stew over the loss of form and reflect on how unlucky he is and how things never seem to go right for him.

The path to success in any endeavour is always strewn with obstacles and failures, but it's how we react to them that determines the ultimate outcome. Form slumps are actually periods where Napoleon has taken negative control over Siggy, and a negative snowball effect is in place. The more frequent the failures, the more active Napoleon becomes; and the more active Napoleon becomes, the more frequent the failures. Napoleon, confronted by the pressure of competition with the instinctive options of fight or flight, succumbs to his fears and runs away. He ducks the competitive situation with all its perceived risks. He loses form.

The one thing Napoleon can't overcome, however, is the desire and determination to win that drives the player with the positive mental attitude. The road to mastery of any skill or sport is never-ending. Time and again we will fail but, if there was an end to the road, there'd be nothing left to achieve. Desire would diminish together with the enjoyment of the challenge, and it would be pointless to carry on.

No one completely masters their Napoleon, and as long as they don't there'll always be the carrot at the end of the stick to motivate them in their pursuit of excellence. They'll continue to fail from time to time, but will interpret failure as an opportunity to learn, to feed more pure and uncluttered data into Siggy. As long as they maintain this attitude, they'll continue to improve.

To understand the mechanics of loss of form, we'll look at the case of a player—we'll call him George—who started out in the game with a hiss and a roar, to the degree that within a couple of seasons of leaving high school he was being picked for a representative team whose players were mostly older than himself. He initially responded well to the bigger and tougher opposition he met at this higher level, and it looked as if his star was on the rise. The next year he was an automatic choice for the same team which, because he was now heavier and more mature, confidently expected him to maintain, if not improve, his form of the previous season.

But from the start of the new season George, a loose forward, ran into problems with his tackling. Playing against bigger men the previous year had made him tentative in the tackle, and even though he took the field each time determined never to flinch from his defensive obligations, there always seemed to be that fatal split second of hesitation in his approach that gave the ball-carrier the opportunity to off-load, stay standing in the tackle or evade him altogether.

This sort of situation is food and drink to Napoleon and, before George knew what was happening, he was trying too hard and mistiming his tackles from all angles. The harder he tried the worse he played, and he ended up being dropped back to club competition after only two more representative games.

George took this pretty hard because he felt he'd let down not only himself, but his team-mates and his province as well. He just wished he could find a rock to crawl under—and the negative snowball effect was under way. He was on the run instead of staying to fight.

Come the next season, George produced more inconsistent tackling performances and, even though he wasn't doing too badly in other facets of his game, he no longer enjoyed the challenge of making tackles. Opponents began to suspect they could run through him. George began to expect to miss tackles. Siggy, of course, reacted as he always does and duly fulfilled George's expectations: George was becoming a defensive liability.

By the end of that miserable season George had decided that if he was going to stay with the sport he'd have to do something in the off season about his tackling problems, and also about the negative feelings that crowded in on him every time he lined up an opposition ball-carrier. He decided to give it one more go the next year. In the off season he happened to meet an old retired first-class player who'd seen him play two years earlier, and he told George he was 'All Black material'. This chance vote of confidence fired George up, and he began his next season with renewed vigour.

Gradually the situation began to reverse, and by the end of that season he was back in the frame of representative selection. Just being under consideration again for higher honours encouraged him, and George's tackling form began to improve from match to match.

What had happened was that he'd been through the full snowball-effect cycle, from good form to bad and back to good again, from positive to negative to positive. The real problem was that George didn't understand what had happened to him and, as his star went back on the rise again, he began to worry that his improved form wouldn't last.

He was right, of course: having told his Siggy that he couldn't trust himself to maintain his good form, his Siggy responded accordingly, and within another year George had lost his confidence again and quit the game.

George was a sad loss to the game because he'd shown real talent for it. The saddest part was that, had he understood the dynamics of form loss and how to reverse it, he might well have gone on to fulfil the old player's assessment of him as All Black material.

The important thing about form losses is that they can be reversed. Form—good or bad—is not the accident of mind or upbringing that George mistakenly thought it was. Rather, form is a function of the relationship between Napoleon and Siggy. In George's case, Napoleon had far too much to say, putting successive negative and positive spins on the data he was feeding through to Siggy. George's emotional roller coaster could have been brought to a halt.

George's problem could be traced back to that first instance when he flinched in the face of a tackle against a bigger opponent. It wasn't that George was cowardly—if he were he wouldn't have taken up the game in the first place. George wasn't really scared of the big fellow coming at him: what George was scared of was failure. His mistake was to allow his Napoleon to add an irrelevance to the package of data it was sending through to Siggy. As any good tackler will tell you, the size of the ball-carrier is irrelevant. Good tackling technique will overcome size any time—'The bigger they come, the harder they fall' as the saying goes. But George's Napoleon, who had dutifully practised awareness of the ball-carrier's direction and speed relative to George's, then added the useless information that the ball-carrier was also big. Siggy cannot ignore any part of the information he gets from Napoleon, and when he heard the ball-carrier was a big bloke, he was obliged to mix that information with the material on good tackling technique that George had stored on his hard disk through hours of practice. The result? Good technique plus bad data equalled muffed tackles. And George was at the mercy of the snowball effect, which ultimately drove a promising player out of the game.

George's sad experience was a classic, if somewhat extreme, case of his Napoleon and his Siggy performing exactly as they're designed to, but delivering entirely the wrong outcome. Over the next few chapters we'll develop a series of practical exercises designed to ensure that, unlike George's, your Napoleon will pass on only relevant, pure and uncluttered data to Siggy.

Of all the various mental techniques and systems adopted by top sportspeople to optimise their performance, there's one you just can't do without. It's the art of goal-setting, and we'll look at that next.

—5—
Goal-setting

> It is common sense to take a method and try it. If it fails, admit it frankly and try another. But above all, try something. FRANKLIN D. ROOSEVELT

Research shows that the top 10 per cent of achievers, in any field of human endeavour, are goal-setters. You hear it from all top sportspeople—from Beatrice Faumuina to Sebastian Coe, from Kapil Dev to Pat Cash, from Michael Jordan to Mel Meninga, from Grant Fox and John Hart to Shane Howarth and Graham Henry. They all say repeatedly that without goal-setting you couldn't motivate yourself to achieve anything.

But there's a big difference between goal-setting and just fantasising. You can daydream all you like about reaching a World Cup rugby final, but that's not going to get you into one. Wishful thinking is not goal-setting. How do you tell the difference? Simple: goal-setters write their goals down. Wishful thinkers never get that far. And what prompts goal-setters to write things down is desire.

Let's look closer at this first and vital step in mind-training, because everything else flows from it. There's a clear link that we need to establish between goal-setting and desire. They depend on each other, grow from each other.

As we've seen, the main factor in improving your game is developing the ability to feed Siggy ever more pure and uncluttered data while, at the same time, keeping Napoleon's negative influences under control. To feed Siggy all the correct data he needs, we have to concentrate all our attention, freed from external distractions, on how the match we're playing in is developing, and on the rapid adjustments we need to make to maximise our contribution to it.

Concentrating on this ensures Napoleon becomes the perfect computer operator, feeding our computer (Siggy) with an unceasing flow of pure and uncluttered data. At the moment we resume direct involvement in play, we have to be able to switch Napoleon off and leave it entirely up to Siggy to execute the particular skill or exercise required. As we've seen, rugby is a stop-start game, and Napoleon's job is to practise awareness during the stops, then turn everything over to Siggy during the starts.

The problem is that this on-again off-again cycle of gathering information and then putting it into practice takes a level of concentration that can be sustained only if the desire to perform well is high.

How often have you heard rugby commentators say, as a tense encounter reaches its climax, 'Now it's down to whichever side most wants to win'? And they're right. All other things being equal, the winner is always the person with the greatest desire to win.

Now let's not confuse desire with desperation. Desire is a controlled and realistic focus on achieving a pre-set goal. Desperation is mere fear, another manifestation of the flight-or-fight syndrome, a brief and passing surge of motivation. Desire is confidence. Desperation is panic.

In a tight match the player whose desire is strong will stand out as being more relaxed, concentrating more 'in the now', and possessing a powerful expectation of winning. To perform well at any given challenge, desire must have been cultivated to a higher level than that of your competition. This isn't a matter of luck, or the accidents of your upbringing. True desire is not a passive or 'received' quality. It's an active and acquired one.

Sure, desire starts out with an idea, one that lodges in the mind and grows there to a certain degree of its own accord. But there comes a point when that spontaneous desire has to be coldly evaluated by the mind, by the reason, and a decision has to be made as to whether to elevate it to the status of a conscious goal, or leave it to vegetate as a fantasy.

That choice is a conscious and active one, not a passive or subconscious one. It involves a deliberate decision, as distinct from a wishful thought. No one knows better than Grant Fox the difference between the fantasy of becoming a world-renowned rugby player and the reality of it. Fox's first step in establishing himself as one of the greatest rugby players ever was in taking the conscious decision to elevate his desire to be a great player above all the other desires clamouring for his attention.

The rugby player whose desire is high doesn't lose his concentration, or stumble into the trying-harder mode when things aren't going his way. He trusts that as long as he keeps providing Siggy with accurate data, he *must* be putting pressure on his opponents—and should they loosen up at any stage, he's ready and eager to pounce.

Most rugby players turn up to play every weekend with no particular desire in mind except to do all right by the team, and maybe pull off a win. If they don't play well it doesn't matter too much because there's always next weekend. The result is that sometimes they succeed, but whenever they run into opponents with equal—or even lesser—ability, but with a greater desire to win, they're in trouble. They become aimless. Their play loses direction and purpose. The team may experience success every now and then, but the individual player doesn't enjoy it as much as the goal-setting player who gets satisfaction from achieving something he deliberately set out to achieve, whether or not the other members of the team helped or hindered. In rugby, you don't have to be on the winning side to play to your potential and gain huge satisfaction from your performance. Being in a winning team sure helps, but at the end of the day each of us is in charge of only one consciousness—our own—and you don't need the rest of the team to play well, for you to perform brilliantly.

It's a bit like the difference between the person who makes a million dollars by hard work and application, and the one who wins it at Lotto. The one who will really appreciate the million dollars, and will look after it and enjoy it most, is the one who's worked for it. Which explains why so many Lotto winners blow their windfall on one big splurge and end up financially poorer for the experience. The difference between the two is the level of desire they began with. The Lotto winner had a freak win against near-impossible odds. The goal-setter was always backing a certainty.

To perform well at any given challenge, you have to cultivate your desire—very much as a gardener cultivates a plant. The seed may have been planted by chance, but unless it's deliberately cultivated to the exclusion of competing plants around it, it will eventually be overtaken by the weeds that are its natural competition. You have to feed your desire, weed it, water it, nurture it, grow it. You cannot sit back and just hope or expect it to develop with time. If you do, your desire will just wither like an untended plant, eventually die, and be replaced by another plant equally short-lived.

Desire begins as a spontaneous notion, but it survives and flourishes only if it is cultivated. And sportspeople succeed at the highest level only if they cultivate their plant of desire to the exclusion of all others.

Now you may not want to exclude all the other considerations in your life—family, career, other interests—and you don't have to. That's up to you, just as how you use this book is up to you. You can use it just to improve your overall quality and enjoyment of play. You can use it just to get the jump on the other ageing crocks and crooks in a one-off Golden Oldies match, or to target and outplay your marker in the contest to be noticed by the selectors. Or you can use it to become a famous international player. But understand that if you make this last choice, as Grant Fox did, you will have to cultivate your desire to the exclusion of all others.

Whatever your ultimate goal, this book tells you how to achieve it. But even if you only want to stand out in that one-off game, or to beat that one particular opponent you're marking, you have to actively and positively cultivate the desire to do so.

The first step in doing that—in separating true desire from idle fantasy—is to write your goal(s) down. The reason for this is very simple: your mind is chock-full of desires at any given moment: the desire to eat, the desire to rest, the desire for sex, the desire to have all your worries taken care of. These desires are with you all the time. So if you have a special desire, one you really want to realise, you've somehow got to set it apart from the myriad everyday desires clamouring for your attention. And the way to set your special desire apart is to write it down.

Indeed, this leads us to the very definition of success—which is the progressive achievement of personal, written goals. If you're not progressing in a sport as fast as you think you ought to be, the first question you should ask yourself is, 'Have I written down my goals?' And if you haven't, you know immediately why you're not getting anywhere.

Setting goals for yourself and writing them down sends a clear message to Siggy that you mean business. It gives substance to your important desires, setting them above the unimportant ones.

When the opportunity arises to achieve a particular goal, and your desire is high, you can sustain your concentration not just for the first ten minutes of the game, but for the entire match. With written goals you have physical evidence, and a concrete reference point, of your own desire to win. From that point there's so much that flows naturally: you are motivated to win and, to assure yourself of the best possible chance of winning, you become quietly confident and have a high expectation of winning.

The path to success for the goal-setting rugby player becomes a progression of achieving one goal after another, each new one more demanding—and more satisfying—than the last. With written goals the player crystallises his thinking, and begins to plan the desired progress as if on a map. As the player moves along this path, the ultimate goal set at the beginning—and which seemed so distant at the time—comes closer and closer until the day arrives when the destination has been reached.

Then there's the enormous personal satisfaction you gain from writing the word 'achieved' over a written goal. Each time you do it you get a tingle—of delight, of pleasure, of pride (call it what you like but, like love, you only know it when you find it). Whatever name you attach to it, it comes down to it being the comfort and security of knowing you've taken another step along the path towards your ultimate target.

Written goals are the first expression of your desire. Whether it's the written goal or the desire that comes first doesn't really matter. What does matter is that, with written goals and desire, you've got your foot on the first step of the path to success.

Now, let's get down to the business end of goal-setting. First we need to identify a starting point because, to achieve something later, you've got to know where you are now. The best way of identifying your starting point is to write down a summary of where you stand in the sport at the moment. By this we mean your strengths and weaknesses, what you enjoy most about your rugby, what you like least. Your summary should include a description of the best game you ever played, and the best contribution you ever made to a winning match. Note how you felt during your best game or while executing your best kick or line-out take or whatever. What satisfaction did this give you?

This exercise will, in the medium to long term, be immensely revealing to you. It'll teach you things about yourself you never knew you knew. Most importantly, it will be the base point for the charting of your improvement. The act of writing down your personal rugby history makes you think seriously about the game. It makes it easy for you to recognise your strengths (we all have them), and identify the weaknesses (we all have them too) that you'll have to work on. Writing about how you felt when you were performing at your best reaffirms your capacity for success, and gives your confidence a boost.

Write as much as you can on each topic, and be as blunt as you like. Nobody else has to see what you write—it's strictly personal, this exercise, and keeping it that way will ensure you're honest.

Okay, pen and paper at the ready? Answer each of the following questions:

1. When did you take up rugby?
2. What made you take it up?
3. What did you set out to achieve during your first year in the sport?
4. How do you rate yourself as a player—below average, average or above average?
5. Have you performed better or worse than you expected to?
6. How do you rate
   (a) your defensive skills?
   (b) your attacking skills?
7. What are your particular strengths (e.g. tackling, taking high catches)?
8. What are your weaknesses?
9. Which do you prefer—attack or defence?

10. Do you find yourself able to keep up with the play, or do you find yourself being left behind?
11. What's your temperament like?
    (a) Do you think positively?
    (b) Do you cope well with pressure?
    (c) Do you project an aura of confidence?
    (d Do you react calmly to bad luck, bad bounces, bad refereeing or bad weather?
    (e) How do you approach a match against a weaker team?
    (f) How do you approach a match against a stronger team?
    (g) Do you go through form slumps, or periods of self-doubt?
12. What were the two best matches and two best incidents in which you were involved?
13. How did you feel before, during and after these incidents and matches?
14. What skills give you the greatest satisfaction?
15. What's your best skill (e.g. running with the ball, overpowering opposing front-row players)?
16. How consistent are you at turning on your best skill?
17. What skills are you not so good at?
18. What do you need to do to improve these skills?
19. What game format (fifteens or sevens in union; thirteens, tens or sevens in league) do you prefer, and why?
20. What position do you think is the right one for you at the moment?
21. What position would you like to be playing in a couple of years' time?
22. Do you want to improve your game?
23. How important is improvement to you?

Just by answering all these questions—and writing down the answers—you've already made a significant step forward: you've crystallised your thinking. You've brought yourself and your game into sharper focus.

Question 22 obviously begs the answer 'Yes'—why else would you have bought this book but to improve your game? But asking it was still a useful exercise, because in answering 'Yes' you affirmed your intention to improve, and in doing so gave formal notice to Siggy that better rugby is your immediate goal. And if your answer to Question 23 was 'Very', then you've made another important step by reinforcing your affirmation and its implied instruction to Siggy.

What you've written shows you what you've got to do (it identifies areas for improvement), and what you've already done (it proves you've got potential for improvement). You're now ready to start setting your goals and priorities—and already, just by writing down your experiences in rugby, you've significantly improved your chances of achieving them.

–6–
Goals

> Ah, but a man's reach should exceed his grasp. Else what's a heaven for? ROBERT BROWNING

Anyone who has ever embarked on a long-term project knows how rapidly the first flush of enthusiasm melts away as the hours merge into days and the days into weeks. Yet that first flush of enthusiasm is so exciting—you can almost taste your satisfaction at achieving your goal, no matter how distant.

So wouldn't it be great to be able to sustain that excitement? Instead, what tends to happen is that it burns out, leaving you with just a sense of the immensity—even the impossibility—of your goal, and a crushing vision of the gulf between where you are now and where you ultimately want to be.

Well, that initial excitement can be made permanent. It can be locked into your consciousness so that it's an ever-present part of your life, and you need never lose it. The trick lies in nurturing and cultivating your original enthusiasm and excitement, in much the way that a gardener nurtures and cultivates a tiny seed into a great tree. This state of permanent excitement about your goal is what sportspeople refer to as being focused.

And the way you achieve it is by first organising your goals into three distinct tiers: short-term goals, intermediate goals and the ultimate goal. You could call this your hierarchy of goals. Like all hierarchies it's shaped like a triangle, with one single goal at the top (the ultimate goal), a few in the middle (the intermediate goals), and a lot at the bottom (the short-term goals).

Looking at this hierarchy from the bottom up, you quickly see that the process of achieving goals is one of taking small and regular steps towards a preplanned outcome. The 'small and regular steps' are the short-term goals, and the 'preplanned outcome' is the ultimate goal. In between there are intermediate goals.

Broadly speaking, the ultimate goal is the lifetime plan (whatever stage of your life you happen to have reached), the intermediate goal is the year-by-year plan, and the short-term goal is the day-to-day one. Put them all together and you have a master plan.

These three types of goals, formulated into a master plan, give you both the structure and the momentum to achieve. They both generate and maintain that vital excitement about the ultimate goal. Once separated into their three categories, your goals work for you as a simple progression, like a stepladder: work through your short-term goals and they yield an intermediate one. From there you set your sights on your next intermediate goal, and you progress towards it by way of a new set of short-term ones. By working your way like this through your list of intermediate goals, you eventually reach your ultimate goal—the apex of the pyramid. Depending on the scope of your ultimate goal, you could approach it by way of a dozen or more intermediate ones, each of them in turn approached by a series of possibly hundreds of short-term ones.

Structuring your goal-setting in this way delivers momentum, which is your constant sense of direction towards an ultimate goal, your constant excitement with the process of achieving. With this structure it doesn't matter how far away the ultimate goal is—years, decades even—because the achievement of every little short-term goal reinforces your sense of progress, and reduces a vast and complex achievement to a series of small and readily achievable ones.

The golden rules of goal-setting

Before we get down to the practical exercise of defining our goals, we need to take a look at the seven basic rules for setting goals, be they short-term, intermediate or ultimate goals. These are:

Rule 1: Goals must be written down

Merely thinking about goals isn't enough. Thinking keeps them in the realm of fantasy, just another in the smorgasbord of daydreams and brief obsessions that drive us from day to day. The physical act of writing your goals down lifts them out of the world of make-believe, makes them achievable, and spurs you into action. Dreamers never achieve anything. If you really want something you must act—now—and set in train the sequence of actions that will eventually lead to success.

Rule 2: Goals must be written in a positive way

If you're serious about changing your attitude for the better, you can't afford to have a negative thought. If the goal is to improve your goal-kicking, then it must be written down positively. Don't write, 'I will not lift my head as I strike the ball.' That 'not' is a negative, and there's no place for negatives in our scheme of things. Instead, write, 'My goal is to strike the ball smoothly and fluidly.'

Rule 3: Goals must be realistic and attainable

It would be silly to set a goal of representing your country in your first year in the game. In this case the goal itself might conceivably be physically achievable, but the time-frame is patently unrealistic because to achieve it you've first got to take the eye of your national selectors—and they're not even going to look at you till you've got at least a couple of seasons of consistent high performance at the provincial or professional level behind you. This isn't to say that goals need to be cautious or conventional—far from it. But they've got to be realistically achievable, and that includes setting them into a realistic time-frame.

Rule 4: Goals must represent a target not already achieved

There's no satisfaction in achieving again something you've achieved before—unless, of course, circumstances have made a repeat performance vastly more difficult second time round. The idea is to improve—be it to improve yourself, your game, or your life. Goals are the blueprint for raising your standards beyond anything you've done before. For goals, look up, not down. This doesn't mean that if you've been dropped from a team it's not worth setting yourself the goal of getting back into it: if anything, regaining a lost place in a team is harder than being selected for it the first time.

Rule 5: Goals must take personality changes into account

Most of us go through periods of self-doubt. Eliminating them takes time, and this has to be reflected in the goal-setting exercise. You've got to be able to believe in your goals as your point of stability, of certainty, even as you ride the day-to-day roller coaster of your emotions. Goals need to take account of the development of your personality, your self-confidence, your self-image, up to the moment that you set them. Part of the process of moving towards your goals is being able to take increasingly large steps with increasing confidence, but if right now you become a gibbering bundle of nerves the moment you pick up your gear bag, don't assume that's going to change just because you've decided to be an international player instead of a club hack. To make the international grade, you're going to have to work your way through the factors—your onset of nerves when you pick up your gear bag, for example—that limit you at present. Don't kid yourself there are no such limitations there in the first place. You have to recognise them before you can face them; you have to face them before you can change them.

Rule 6: There must be a burning desire to achieve your goals

Unless you're vitally interested in achieving your goals, there's little point in setting them. Goal-setting is about turning yourself from a thinker into a doer. Your goals should be something you're driven to, not just things that take your fancy for the moment. How do you know when you're driven? It's a bit like being in love—hard to describe, but impossible not to recognise once you're in it. It's a combination of magic and certainty. In love the certainty arises from your natural genetic urge to be in love (as a step towards reproducing yourself), and the magic is the indefinable chemistry that starts boiling inside you when you're with the one you love. Potential ultimate goals can be put to the same test as potential love-for-life relationships. You ask yourself, 'Knowing me as I do, and knowing my goal to the degree that I do, can I see us sticking together come what may?' If the answer is 'Yes', you've got yourself a worthwhile ultimate goal.

Rule 7: You must be determined to achieve your goals

Goals don't achieve themselves: you've got to get out there and achieve them. Setbacks, like injury and non-selection, must be expected and surmounted. Disappointments and failures have to be perceived as opportunities to progress, through experience, to the realisation of each goal in turn. Achieving goals inevitably involves rejecting other options which may seem attractive at the time. You have to be prepared to make sacrifices. The techniques in this book are aimed at minimising the sense of loss that making sacrifices entails, and heightening the permanent sense of excitement that closing in on a goal induces. But with the best organisation in the world, you're still going to encounter those moments when you ask yourself 'Is it really worth it?' Having determination means the answer to that question will always be 'Yes'.

Defining your goals

In any goal-setting exercise your starting point is your ultimate goal. In its highest form, this is the real big-picture stuff, the sort of thing of which dreams are made. The ultimate goal can be the one that shapes your life, the focal point of your existence. Alternatively, it can be a goal of limited duration—say, a couple of years away. The important thing is that it's the apex of the triangle of intermediate and short-term goals.

Rugby may or may not be the focal point of this ultimate goal—rugby can be the means to an end, or the end in itself. That's up to you. But you need to have an ultimate goal that gives direction and perspective to your sport.

By its nature, your ultimate goal might seem far-fetched, even a bit crazy, if you were to parade it in front of your friends and family. 'My ultimate goal is to be in a Rugby World Cup championship winning team', or, 'My ultimate goal is to become prime minister, and I intend using the disciplines I develop at rugby to get me there'. Say such things out loud and your best friends might start looking round for the folks in the white coats coming to cart you away to somewhere safe. But don't let that stop you nominating a goal that, on the face of it, might have more than a little element of fantasy to it. Nobody else need see or hear what your ultimate goal is, so there's no need to feel embarrassed about writing it down.

And who's to say you're not going to achieve your ultimate goal anyway, no matter how lofty it may seem? Somebody has to make up the numbers in a team that wins the world championship; somebody has to be prime minister. Why not you? Grant Fox achieved his goal, and a whole lot more besides, and he began by writing down his ultimate goal long before there was a Rugby World Cup to aspire to. He wasn't rash enough to tell anyone about it at the time, but he chose the ultimate goal of becoming an All Black, and he wrote it down as such. He finally got there by a succession of small steps, of short-term and intermediate goals, but his ultimate goal was what gave him his sense of direction.

Once you've worked out what your own ultimate goal is, write it down. This is item one on your master plan. Write your ultimate goal down and you've just taken the first—and arguably the most important—step in your quest for excellence.

Now for the next step. If your ultimate goal was representing your country at rugby, you'd have to make it into a good provincial or professional team as a preliminary to national selection. Before you get into a provincial or professional team, there are regional and sub-union selection honours to be won. Before you can win regional or sub-union selection you've got to make a name for yourself at the local and club levels. And to do that you've got to get your attitude right.

All this reinforces the notion that before the ultimate goal can be achieved, you've got to work your way through a succession of intermediate and short-term goals. Intermediate goals are the major steps between you and the realisation of your ultimate goal. Again, taking the case of our wannabe international player, intermediate goals would progress through club, sub-union, provincial and professional teams, to national ones and national selection. Your first goal, for example, might be the club 1st XV, and you'd want at least

Selectors are the gatekeepers to rugby players' advancement: here the selectors keeping the All Black gate are (from left) Peter Thorburn, Alex Wyllie and John Hart. Non-selection, no less than selection, should be viewed as an insight into what the selectors are looking for.

The coach is the principal author of both strategy and tactics, and it's vital for the player to get to know how the coach views his particular role in the context of the overall plan. The coach is this case is Graham Henry, in the days when, with Grant Fox at first five-eighth, he was guiding Auckland to near-invincibility.

There may be 60,000 spectators in the stands, and millions more watching on television, but the individual player must be focused on performing his particular set of skills just as well whether anyone's watching or not. Here Sean Fitzpatrick prepares to throw into a line-out during a 1992 New Zealand-South Africa test, against the backdrop of a packed stadium.

Rugby's a stop-start game, with Siggy doing the business spontaneously during the starts, and Napoleon contributing awareness and gathering information during the stops—especially during the unwelcome stops like the one pictured here, where the opposition has scored a try and is about to attempt the conversion.

Individual positional skill-sets, like those being demonstrated by All Black lock Norm Maxwell in a line-out against South Africa, are stored as ready-access skill-files in your personal inbuilt computer, your Siggy.

Total commitment to the execution of a skill—here demonstrated by an Argentinian Puma in tackling All Black flanker Taine Randell—is the logical expression of that most basic of human emotions, fear of physical hurt. Danger and fear are minimised by precise and committed execution of practised skills. Anything less than total commitment and surgical precision invites injury.

The side-step, here being executed by Scottish first five-eighth Craig Chalmers against the All Blacks (playing in their white strip), is the result of a decision made in a fraction of a second by the player's personal inbuilt computer. Siggy's ability to make quick decisions literally on the run is heightened by visualisation exercises, which ensure the necessary skill-files are at his fingertips.

one such intermediate goal per year projecting you towards your ultimate goal. Especially in the early stages of your overall plan, you might want more intermediate goals. That's fine, and it's best to err on the side of too many rather than too few intermediate goals, but remember that these are the big stepping stones, not to be confused with the day-to-day items that comprise short-term goals.

Once you've sorted out your intermediate goals, write them on a chart in descending order below your ultimate goal—that is, your last intermediate goal goes immediately below your ultimate goal, and your first intermediate goal goes at the bottom. Write beside each goal the approximate date—it may just be a particular year—by which you want to have achieved it. Leave room alongside each goal to write in the actual date and occasion on which you achieved each successive intermediate goal.

This chart is your master plan. Pin it up in a place where you're going to see it often. This might be your bedroom wall or, if you want to be even more private about it, on the inside of your cupboard door or desk drawer. Wherever you put it, it's got to be somewhere that you'll see it regularly—several times a day—so that it serves as a constant reminder of the next goal up on your list, and the progress you've made towards achieving it. As a rule of thumb, if you find yourself looking in a mirror more often than you look at your master plan, you've got your priorities back to front.

This constant review of your master plan is a means of giving yourself positive messages both coming and going: you're reminded of the need to achieve the next goal coming up on your list, and your determination to do so is reinforced by the satisfaction of knowing you've got achieved goals behind you.

On page 67 is a typical master plan, as written for someone who wants to play World Cup rugby, but who is still at high school and has yet to make the school 2nd XV. You'll see that alongside each goal is the deadline or time-frame the player has given himself to achieve the goal. Establishing a time-frame prevents procrastination: it reminds you to act now.

What if you miss some of these deadlines? No matter. Failures are part of the learning curve too. A failure will simply increase your determination to carry on climbing the ladder, even if a particular deadline has to be rescheduled because you missed it the first time. 'Failure' to make a deadline must not be viewed as 'failure' in the sense of the collapse of your goals and plans. Rather, it should be perceived as a delay brought about by your having not quite enough knowledge to meet the deadline at the time.

Missing a deadline doesn't mean you've blown the whole effort and might as well give up. It simply means that the deadline wasn't realistic. You get exactly the same message from being ahead of a deadline as from being behind one: namely that the original deadline wasn't realistic (because you achieved it sooner—or later—than you expected). You wouldn't give up just because you achieved something earlier than you expected to—you're more likely to be pleased than sorry—so don't go thinking of giving up if you happen to achieve it a bit later than you expected. Achievement is a factor of knowledge, of pure and uncluttered data fed into Siggy. Being early or late for a deadline simply means the data on which you estimated the deadline wasn't accurate.

Early or late, you've got to readjust your sights, using your ever-increasing knowledge and experience to make your time-frame more realistic. You do this by rewriting your short-term goals to take account of your new knowledge. This in turn makes sure your ultimate goal remains achievable.

Another factor to keep in mind is that you're setting goals exclusively for yourself—not for the team you play for. This book and its principles are for the individual rugby player. Psychological preparation of the team as a unit is the responsibility of the coach—or, at the highest levels, the team shrink. This book is aimed at the individual who wants to achieve in rugby irrespective of whether the rest of the individuals in his team share the same goals.

The master plan below has been drafted to span a period of ten years, mainly to illustrate the considerable time-frame that could (and perhaps should) be reflected in the formulation of your ultimate goal and your steady progression towards it. The assumption in this case is that you're starting in your late teens and you've got a playing life of at least ten years in which to achieve your ultimate goal. There have been famous exceptions but, generally, if you haven't made it into your national team by the time you're 30, you're not going to make it. This is by no means to suggest that this book and the principles it espouses will work for you only if you're

Master Plan

Goal	Deadline	Date achieved	Event
World Cup champion (ultimate goal)	2011		
National selection	2010		
Professional	2008		
National Emerging Players Squad	2007		
National Colts (under-21 side)	2006	August	NPC
Sub-union (regional)	2005	October	Town v Country
Club Senior A	2005	May	Local derby
Club Senior B	2005	March	Season opener
Provincial Youth grade	2004		
Club Youth A grade	2004	March	Season opener
Club Youth B grade	2003	March	Season opener
High school 1st XV	2002	March	Season opener
High school 2nd XV	2001	March	Season opener

still in your teens. You could be the ageing 30-something battler who can see the end of your senior club career coming into view, and you want to go out with a bang by getting a few games for the sub-union or regional side. By all means create a master plan with a time-span of just a couple of seasons—even a single season. By the same token you might be a real youngster playing at primary school level, or a hoary ancient in his seventies wondering if he couldn't still turn something on for the Golden Oldies. The time-span of the master plan is less important than the principle of master planning. Adjust the example on the next page to suit your individual circumstances.

As an example of a master plan, this one is deliberately simplistic in that, until the year 2004, our imaginary goal-setter achieves all his intermediate goals in their correct time sequence. Then he skips making his provincial youth grade team because, say, those selectors don't like him, but he moves on up to Senior B club play the next year anyway. In reality, rugby being the sort of game it is and advancement being dependent on the vagaries of different selectors at different levels, the achievement of goals will almost certainly be less of a straight-line progression than the example below. But no matter. Our goal-setter has leap-frogged one intermediate goal in achieving a higher one—he's that much closer to his ultimate goal of the World Cup. Don't fear that leap-frogging goals is going to wreck your entire master plan—instead, welcome it as a short cut. The thing about team sports like rugby is that the moment you get picked for a higher team, you can pat yourself on the back for cutting the mustard in all the lower grades, even if you didn't actually get to play in them: you can be pretty sure that once you've been selected for a higher-grade team, the teams below you would be delighted to have you even if they overlooked you when you were available for them. Your missing out back then was their mistake, not yours.

Your master plan, containing your intermediate goals leading up to your ultimate goal, is your blueprint for success. It's a map of the future which acts as a constant reminder to you of the progress you've made in your search for excellence. You look at it, consult it, are actively aware of it several times a day—hence the need to keep it in a place where you'll encounter it routinely and often (preferably without anyone else laying eyes on it).

Master plans are personal things, and each individual's plan is different from everyone else's. The one above is designed to fit the classic situation of the teenage player with all his top rugby still ahead of him. But, as we pointed out earlier, the principles apply equally well to the primary school child just starting out in the game, or the aged warhorse keen to make a comeback at the social or Golden Oldies level. In between those two parameters there's a growing number of players of all ages and both sexes to whom rugby is no longer just a young man's game. Recent years have seen the spectacular emergence of women's international rugby with its own World Cup (won in 1998 by New Zealand), lower age group internationals (as young as under-15s), and a professional slant being put on the notion of Golden Oldies rugby by dedicated semi-professional former international players. It probably won't be long before there are age-group international tournaments for everyone from early teenagers to 70-year-olds.

The United States has a long history of dominating women's rugby, and Japan has been showing the way for years in making rugby a game for the middle-aged and elderly as much as for the young. The leading rugby countries of both hemispheres are following the American and Japanese leads, and it's not beyond the realms of possibility that a multiracial rugby version of basketball's Harlem Globetrotters could make an appearance within the next few years.

There's an important message in this: success is measured by your performance as a factor of your potential. A person who has the potential to run a mile in four minutes, but who fails to do so, is less successful than the one who has the potential to run a mile in only five minutes but, after a lot of trying, finally achieves it. There are no absolutes in life: everything is relative to the circumstances in which it occurs.

Having said all that, let's move on from our master plan to the detail of how our would-be World Cup player sets about climbing the ladder of his intermediate goals to his ultimate goal. For the purposes of the exercise we'll make our player a fly half (first five-eighths) with ambitions to follow in Grant Fox's famous footsteps. Don't be put off by your being, say, a front-row forward: you may seldom get the opportunities to kick, pass and choose tactical options the way a fly half has to, but the principles are the same for the block-layer at fly half as they are for the concrete-mixer in the front of the scrum.

The first question the player has to ask himself is, 'Why haven't I already realised the first of my intermediate goals?'—in this case making the school's 2nd XV. He'll have no trouble in finding answers—and here are a few of the most likely ones:

1. I don't have much confidence in my ability.
2. I'm not consistent enough.
3. The opposition's loose forwards seem to get to me at the same time as I receive the ball from the scrum half (halfback).
4. I've played a lot of my rugby in other backline positions, and I'm still coming to terms with the demands of fly half.
5. I pick the wrong option too often—kicking when I should pass, passing when I should kick.
6. Both my positional and place-kicking are inconsistent.

Our player has now established why he has yet to achieve his first intermediate goal. In doing so he's written down as many reasons as he could think of—and there could be a dozen or more rather than just the six we've listed here.

What our player is saying is that if he had more confidence in his ability, was more consistent, less pressured by loosies, more familiar with his chosen position, better at picking the right options and had a more reliable boot, he'd be elevated to the 2nd XV. In short, he's quantified his problem.

His next step is to go to each reason and assign to it a short-term goal aimed at remedying that particular problem. Given the problems outlined above, the following short-term goals suggest themselves:

1. To grow his self-confidence.
2. To become more consistent.
3. To get the loosies off his back.
4. To better understand the demands of the fly half position.
5. To refine his option-taking.
6. To polish his kicking techniques.

In the context of the 10-year master plan that our player has outlined for himself, six short-term goals is not many—especially when you see that he's got more than twice as many intermediate goals. But short-term goals are different from the ultimate and intermediate goals, in that you revise them weekly. More on those weekly revisions later. For now, let's concentrate on this first list of short-term goals and see where they might lead us.

Write down the short-term goals again and, after each, write strategies for addressing them. At the end of the exercise, the following might be what our ambitious player would have written:

1. To grow my self-confidence:
   (a) I'll write an affirmation (covered in the next chapter) aimed at attacking my self-doubt and fear of failure.
   (b) I'll check the local library for self-improvement books.

2. To improve the consistency of my performance:
   (a) I'll develop creative visualisation exercises (covered in Chapter 8).
   (b) I'll check the local library for books by top players in my position.

3. To get the loosies off my back:
   (a) I'll watch videos of top loose forwards in action to see where they're coming from.
   (b) I'll seek advice as to whether I'm creating my problems by myself, or . . .
   (c) Whether slow delivery of the ball by the scrum half is what's making me an easy target for the loosies.

4. To better understand the demands of my chosen position.

5. To refine my option-taking:
   (a) I'll watch the 1st XV's fly half and work out what he's doing that I'm not.
   (b) I'll study a coaching manual to improve my understanding of my responsibilities.
   (c) I'll watch videos of the top fly halves in the world to see how they handle given situations.
   (d) I'll develop default options—automatic responses—to given situations.

6. To polish my kicking techniques:
   (a) I'll seek advice from the best kicking coach or player in the district.
   (b) I'll practise by myself at least three hours a week.
   (c) I'll run videos of the best kickers in the world frame-by-frame.

What's beginning to emerge here is that short-term goals become the basis for your daily schedule of activities towards your next (or first) intermediate goal.

Different sports require different training schedules. Runners, for example, have a daily schedule that prescribes the sorts of distances they must cover, and the effort (speed) at which to cover them. It's our contention that this sort of training schedule can be a daunting thing, especially if you see it stretching away months in advance. There's not much room to adjust them to meet the particular needs of the individual. These one-size-fits-all schedules are particularly inappropriate for team sports, such as rugby, where each position creates a different set of demands and responsibilities for each player.

Accordingly, the principle we espouse in this book is that you recast your concept of a training schedule into a succession of short-term goals. Training schedules and short-term goals fairly quickly merge into pretty much the same thing. The difference is that where training schedules tend to be rigid, long-term and burdensome, short-term goals are flexible, immediate and satisfying. The difference really is one of attitude—and getting your attitude right is what this book is all about.

With this in mind, you can now expand your list of short-term goals into a week-by-week activity list. Set yourself a particular time every week—it'll take no more than half an hour—and sit down and write out a daily list of activities based on your written short-term goals. Taking the typical six goals listed above, your week's activity list—excluding fitness training and team practices—would begin to look something like this:

Monday: Meet coach for work-sessions—ten minutes each on punts, drop kicks and place kicks; practise one hour alone; read about the demands of your particular position from the coaching manual; do the mind exercises—those covered in later chapters and the two described below—just before going to sleep.

Tuesday: Practise one hour alone before team training; watch video of a major international; do the mind exercises just before going to sleep.

Wednesday: Meet coach for 30-minute work-session on kicking; write down a list of the main tactical options outlined in the coaching manual, and write a short sentence on when to use each; do your mind exercises just before going to sleep.

Thursday: Practise kicking alone for one hour before team training; read the first couple of chapters of a top fly half's memoirs; do the mind exercises just before going to sleep.

Friday: Practise kicking alone for one hour; watch a video of a first-class or international game; revise your tactical options and when to employ them; do the mind exercises just before you go to sleep.

Saturday: Play your weekly match; concentrate on switching Napoleon on to practise awareness during the lulls in the game, and off to give Siggy a free rein when the game is flowing; just before going to sleep, go over the game again in your mind, highlighting the aspects of it that gave you most satisfaction.

Sunday: Review your use of tactical options during the game the previous day, highlighting your best selections; read a couple more chapters of the top fly half's memoirs; watch a video of a top match; prepare next week's activity list; do the mind exercises just before going to sleep.

You'll be startled how quickly this sort of weekly schedule, supplementing your regular team practices and fitness training, irons out the problems in your game at the same time as it boosts your self-confidence. The results will come fastest at the start of such a schedule, then the rate of improvement will taper off over time—but you'll keep on improving, keep on achieving those intermediate goals as long as you keep up the exercises. The reverse applies if you quit the regime: your rate of decline will be fastest immediately after you quit, and you'll get worse more slowly thereafter. It's just the way that Siggy and Napoleon work. Goal-setting and attainment comprise a progression of simple, daily steps towards a predetermined target, but you always make your biggest strides at the start.

It's that daily sense of achievement, the daily nurturing and cultivating of the excitement of achievement, that will get you where you want to go. You could be a 70-year-old with a two-year project of getting back into the game, or a primary school youngster thinking two decades ahead, or anything in between, but the principles remain the same, and the goals are equally achievable.

Finally, a word about those mind exercises (including the ones you'll learn about in the chapters ahead) to be completed each night, and another to be completed each week. The time to do both these exercises is just before you go to sleep. The reason for this timing is to allow your subconscious to chew over your activities and goals throughout the one-third of your day when you're asleep and can't do it consciously.

So, each night of the week you do two things:

1. Check off each completed activity on the list, adding a few comments on how you went. For example, you might write against your entry for Monday, 'Coach nails down kicking problem to my lifting my head just as I strike the ball. Solution: keep the head still throughout the kicking action.' Friday's might read, 'Yeah, I'm starting to understand which tactical options are the best to employ in which circumstances. The first test of my progress will be the game tomorrow.'

2. Read slowly through your master plan. You're already coming face to face with your master plan several times a day, because you've probably laminated it and posted it in a place you can't help seeing it. The nightly read will consolidate the impact of just seeing it during the day, and your subconscious will involuntarily reinforce the importance of it while you sleep.

Then, every week (ideally Sunday night), after you've prepared the next week's activity list, you must:

1. Review your short-term progress to date. Take special note of any little advances you've made—and don't forget to congratulate yourself. 'That place-kick action of mine is really beginning to smooth itself out, and is feeling sweet', or 'Hey, I gained 60 metres of territory by using the long, deep kick at just the right time—fantastic!'
2. Review your master plan one more time. Think back to the last intermediate goal you achieved, and remember how you felt at the moment you achieved it, what it felt like when you came to check it off on your master plan. Think ahead to the achievement of your next intermediate goal, and how significant a step that will be towards your ultimate goal.

Done all that? Written all those things down? Reviewed them? Slept on them? Congratulations, you're on the road to becoming a real achiever. You've already taken the biggest, hardest and most important steps. From here on success is a matter of small and steady progressions. Now all you need are the mind exercises that will ensure Siggy and Napoleon are constantly operating along the same lines you are.

—7—
Affirmations

I am strong, I am invincible, I am woman.   HELEN REDDY

This whole book focuses on the relationship between Siggy (our personal in-built computer) and Napoleon (our personal in-built computer operator). It's about how Siggy needs to be supplied with pure and uncluttered information, and how we stop Napoleon putting his own negative spin on that information—or, better still (as we're about to see), how we get Napoleon to put a positive spin on it.

In the previous chapter we saw how goal-setting heightens and maintains our excitement so we become ever more focused. This 'focus' is our first way of ensuring that Napoleon feeds Siggy only pure and uncluttered information. It's this focus that becomes so precise over time that Napoleon can tell Siggy to within a fraction of a centimetre how much width and length to put on a place kick and, to a single degree, the direction to kick it in. Grant Fox's Napoleon did this for his Siggy—and together they made him the highest-scoring All Black of his or any previous generation.

Understand that you can never overestimate Napoleon's influence on Siggy, because all the information Siggy needs has to pass through Napoleon first. Napoleon is part of the team, and has a lot more to offer than just being the eyes and the ears. But Siggy's a machine, and will do whatever Napoleon tells him. If Napoleon feeds Siggy garbage information, Siggy delivers garbage results.

Unlike Siggy, Napoleon is far more than a machine: he doesn't just receive and transfer information—he interprets it. And that's where his real power—and weakness—lies. Napoleon can interpret information negatively, and Siggy will respond by delivering exactly the outcome we don't want. Or, conversely, Napoleon can put a positive interpretation on the information he feeds Siggy, and Siggy responds with the outcome we do want. The difference between getting the outcome we do want, and the outcome we don't want, in the end comes down to whether Napoleon puts a positive or a negative spin—or none at all—on the information he gives Siggy.

If we can prevent Napoleon from putting any spin on the information he passes to Siggy, the resultant performance will be fine. But if we can get Napoleon to put a positive spin on the information, the resultant performance may be brilliant. The trick, of course, is to ensure Napoleon puts only a positive spin on the information he sends Siggy. And that's what we're going to try to do.

As we've seen, focus and awareness are the tools we use to ensure Napoleon provides accurate and detailed information. But there's another tool, and it works right alongside. It works not by diverting or eliminating the negative thought patterns in Napoleon's subconscious, but by replacing them with positive ones.

Yes, it's as simple as that. And it's called affirmation.

The famous American motivator, Ziggy Ziggler, put it this way: if somebody came to your home and dumped a bag of rubbish on your floor, you'd be justifiably angry. You'd want the offender to clean up the mess, and you'd tell him he wasn't welcome in your home any more. Why is it then (Ziggy asked) that human beings seem prepared to let people dump the garbage of negative thoughts and ideas in their minds? Good question.

There's a tall poppy syndrome at work in most cultures—you know, it's that tendency to criticise successful people, to be reluctant to experiment with new ideas, and it's that seeming need to have everyone conform to some sort of general mediocrity. The tall poppy syndrome probably exists in every society, but the disease is supposed to be particularly prevalent in New Zealand and Australia, probably because they're relatively 'new' countries and still a bit self-conscious. Be that as it may, it's a negative conditioning that begins at school where children are subject to peer pressure—that is, 'Conform or be unpopular'—and it continues right through adult life.

Remembering that success is what you achieve in relation to

your potential to achieve it, it seems that the people who are most ready to wield the tall poppy axe are those who never succeed in anything much themselves, but feel less uncomfortable about their own failures if they're chopping down people who do succeed.

We've all the heard the 'experts' at the local pub or club putting down Shane 'Fatty' Warne or Gazzer 'The Guzzler' Gascoigne. Of course nobody's above criticism, but people who rubbish the world's best spin-bowling cricketer just because he has to watch his weight, or smirk about a brilliant footballer who may be too much of an individualist for a team game, are themselves almost always talkers rather than doers. They would have us believe that they deserve the winners' accolades precisely because of their own lack of success, rather than the accolades going to the Warnes and Gascoignes of this world for their abundance of it. Ziggy Ziggler was right: if we're prepared to let such self-important losers fill our minds with negative garbage, we might as well let them dump rubbish on our sitting-room floor.

This is where affirmations come in. What they do is screen out the negative garbage we're constantly bombarded with and, instead, let our Napoleons constantly default into positive thought patterns.

Affirmations are positive statements of what we'd like to do or be in the future, but written down in a way that suggests we've already achieved or become them.

Philosophers and achievers throughout history agree that if we continually transmit a positive thought to our subconscious minds, by repeatedly saying something aloud that reflects our desire, that desire will become reality. More than a century ago the French philosopher Émile Coué flatly told people they would feel—and actually be—happier and more successful if they stood in front of a mirror and said out loud twice a day, 'Every day, in every way, I'm getting better and better.' A lot of people laughed at the idea because they couldn't believe that something so simple, so effortless, could have so lasting and favourable an effect on human life. But it does.

You don't believe us? You don't believe the eminent Dr Coué? You don't believe the millions of people who have put this principle to the test in the century since he first expounded it? Then try it yourself. For one month carry out this exercise twice a day, every day. Then bring your smiling face and positive outlook back to this book, and let us make a top rugby player out of you as well. (Alternatively, carry on with the exercises in this book, and save yourself a month of reinventing the psychological wheel.)

It's true: the constant repetition day after day of a positive thought eventually takes root in your subconscious, your Napoleon. It usually takes a minimum of three to four weeks for affirmations to bed themselves into your subconscious—but bed themselves they do.

Affirmations work by constantly reinforcing the changes you want to make in your life. Entire religions are structured round affirmations—some call them prayers, some call them mantras—and every politician knows that if you tell the people something often enough, they'll eventually come to accept it as gospel.

Affirmations are self-fulfilling prophecies. They can work with negative messages no less than with positive ones, but it's the positives that we're interested in here. The more the positive message is imprinted on your subconscious, the closer you get to the message becoming reality.

Outwardly the affirmation doesn't seem to change anything at first, but inwardly it'll be making its imprint on your subconscious. And within 30 days you'll start to see the message expressing itself in your spontaneous thought patterns.

People usually live up to the expectations, good or bad, that other people have of them, but they always live up to the expectations they have of themselves. We are what we think we are. Change a person's perceptions of themselves and you change the person.

When we constantly reinforce an expectation by repeating an affirmation over and over, we begin to expect to see changes in our personality and/or performance, and we begin to act like the person and/or performer we want to become.

It doesn't matter whether or not we believe in the power of affirmations, any more than it matters whether or not we believe in the power of gravity. If we use affirmations constantly we will experience change, no less surely than if we step off a cliff we will begin to travel downwards. Rapidly.

You've only got to go down to your local footy club to observe the power of affirmations. You'll meet people who practise negative ones all the time, and most of us fall into the habit of it at least occasionally. The team place-kicker might say, 'I can't strike the ball right. I can't get the lift I need. I'm forever pulling or slicing it.' These are negative affirmations that, like positive ones, are self-fulfilling prophecies. The more people say they can't strike the ball right, the more it wobbles in the air. The more they say they can't get the lift they need, the flatter the ball's trajectory. The more they say they can't help pulling or slicing the ball, the more drunkenly it lurches away to one side or other of the sticks.

The more we make affirmations, positive or negative, the more accurate they are. Human beings are programmed to live up to their expectations: if we say often enough that we can't do something, we'll prove ourselves absolutely right. But if we say often enough that we *can*, we'll also prove ourselves absolutely right.

What do you want to be? Positive or negative? Successful or unsuccessful? Take your pick.

We've all been conditioned more or less to conform to the average by peer pressure. We accept negative affirmations both from the people we talk to and from our own thought patterns. But the deliberate use of positive affirmations displaces the negative ideas instilled in us over years of conditioning.

It's like dropping coins into a glass full of water: as you do, the water overflows. The more coins we drop in, the less water is left in the glass. Our mind is the glass, negative thoughts are the water, and positive affirmations are the coins we drop in. Just keep dropping those positive thoughts in, and the negative ones are forced out.

How to write affirmations

To create an affirmation you take an intermediate goal (or, as we'll see later, your ultimate goal) and write on a card a positive statement as if you'd already achieved it. Stick it in your wallet, or somewhere you'll come across it often, and read it—preferably out loud—whenever you do. As a minimum you'll need to do it at least half a dozen times a day.

This is a standard technique that professional motivators teach salespeople. For example, you might have a car salesperson who has an intermediate goal of selling two cars a week over a year with the aim of making, say $60,000. He or she would write an affirmation this way: 'I am a top-line car salesperson. I sell over a hundred cars a year and earn over $60,000.'

Sure it works. That's why all these big corporations spend zillions on professional motivators to wind up their salespeople. If the corporations didn't get a decent return on the money they invest in the Ziggy Zigglers of this world, they'd invest it elsewhere.

Having trouble with the way you strike the ball? Want to develop a style where the ball gets away smoothly all the time? Write yourself an affirmation like this: 'I strike the ball with machine-like precision. It feels as though the ball is an extension of my body. It always leaves the tee on an even keel. My action is as smooth as silk.'

Of course, at the time of writing it, the statement isn't true. If it were true you wouldn't need to make it. But this doesn't make the statement a lie, because you're not trying to deceive anyone else. Rather, it's a projection into the future, a Napoleon-conditioning exercise. By constantly reinforcing the change you want, through goal-setting and repetition of the affirmation, the statement must inevitably come true.

One of the most famous affirmations in sports history was written by the coach of the seemingly invincible Notre Dame gridiron team that dominated college football in the United States for years. Long before the American sports industry began to cotton on to the sports psychology that the Iron Curtain countries were already masters of, Notre Dame coach Frank Leahy wrote out this affirmation in huge letters on the changing-room wall, and required every player to read it out loud before going onto the playing field: 'When the going gets tough, the tough get going.' It did and they did too.

No less famous an affirmation was Mohammad Ali's self-fulfilling prophecy: 'I am the greatest.' He was—and probably still is. At the time Ali started using his affirmation he was by no means the greatest. He was just a kid with quick hands and a chip on his shoulder because his 1960 Olympic heavyweight boxing gold medal brought no respect for this black fighter in his hometown, St Louis, Missouri. He went on to parlay his 'I am the greatest' affirmation into three world professional championships over the next fifteen years, despite losing several peak fighting years when banned by the sport's administrators for refusing to fight in the Vietnam War.

Affirmations are mottos or action statements. Writing them, reading them and seeing them every day imprints the attitudes needed for success indelibly on the subconscious mind. At first you may find it hard to accept your affirmation when you know that, at the outset, it hasn't happened—it just plain isn't true. As a kicker you might be all too well aware that your action is lousy, and it seems stupid to be standing in front of a mirror saying out loud how good it is. But constant repetition will have you working on your technique, moving ever closer to getting it perfect, until the day arrives when you can look yourself squarely in the eye, say the words of your affirmation out loud, and know it is now true.

By constantly repeating the statement, you establish the expectation of possessing a great technique, or whatever else you want, and because everyone lives up to the expectations they have of themselves, it's inevitable that the expectation becomes reality.

Let's get back to the rugby player who sets himself the ultimate goal of being part of a world champion team. Let's say he's got an intermediate goal of being picked for his provincial side. Here's the way he might write an affirmation to start using, say, three months before the start of the representative season.

'I have been picked for the provincial representative team. The further I go in the provincial competition, the better I play. I thrive on pressure, and play superbly against top opposition. I'm always relaxed, positive, and totally confident in my inner ability to outperform any opposition I meet.'

At the time he writes the statement, the player may never even have been picked for anything beyond his club side, let alone for a team made up of the best players in the province. But he's got three months to make the statement a self-fulfilling prophecy.

Affirmations can be rigid and long-term—like Ali's 'I am the greatest'—and used from the start of your campaign to the realisation of your ultimate goal. Alternatively, they can be relatively short-term, and geared to your succession of intermediate goals.

Keep in mind that affirmations can't be geared to a short-term goal. This is because it takes a month or so for an affirmation to bed into your subconscious and start affecting your performance.

Thereafter it needs more months—possibly years, depending on your master plan's time-frame—for you to get the full value of this lighthouse in the darkness of your subconscious.

Where you create an affirmation to serve you long-term, such as for your ultimate goal, it should be short and general. For the medium term, such as for an intermediate goal, the affirmation can be longer and quite specific. Generally speaking, the longer the term of your campaign, the more general the affirmation can be. If you've got the ultimate goal of being in the team that wins the Rugby World Cup in the year 2011, 'I am part of the world champion side of 2011' is about as specific an affirmation as you need for a decade-long campaign. By the end of that period, if you say it out loud and sincerely to your own face twice a day, you'll believe it all right—and it'll probably be true.

If you're looking at making a provincial or national team, or have a similar intermediate goal at least three months down the track, your affirmation needs to be longer and more specific, as in: 'I am in the provincial representative side. The nearer I get to my goal, the more relaxed and confident I become. I particularly relish the underdog role outplaying big-name players.'

Let's briefly review where we've got to so far. You've now put in place two of the three main mental tools you require for playing better rugby simply by thinking. First you had the goal-setting—definitely the most important. Now you've got affirmation—a secondary but no less vital tool. Already you've got the basic tools for success in rugby or in any sport, and exercising them takes you only a few minutes each day.

If you were to describe goal-setting as the horse, affirmations would be the saddle and bridle. In the next chapter we'll introduce you to the jockey, the third of the core ingredients of performance enhancement by mind-training.

—8—
Creative visualisation

> You can have anything you can imagine yourself as having. HENRY FORD

Sure, it's hard to read out loud an affirmation you know to be untrue. 'I'm the greatest'? 'My kicking action is as smooth as silk'? Napoleon has heaps to say on the subject: 'Who do you think you are, making statements like this when you know they're not true? If anyone heard you they'd think you were nuts. Are you the full biscuit anyway?'

We can overcome Napoleon's scepticism by using him in a positive rather than a negative way. We know that Napoleon—our imaginative computer operator—deals in things past and future. We also know that he's just as important to us as Siggy, our personal in-built computer. Without Napoleon we have no desire, no dreams to fulfil. Life would be awfully boring. Without Napoleon we couldn't enjoy success, couldn't experience disappointment. And if we use Napoleon in a positive fashion we can get him to create pictures of the future, and transfer them to the present.

What we do is use Napoleon like a video or movie camera to show Siggy, in perfect detail and vivid colour, exactly what an affirmation will look like when it comes to pass. Let's look at that affirmation on kicking: 'I have an action that's smooth as silk.' Just saying it out loud will eventually bed it into your subconscious, but your brain reacts better to pictures than to words. Remember that saying, 'A picture is worth a thousand words'? It's true, all right.

Using mind-pictures in conjunction with affirmations makes your imagination work positively for you. Picturing and feeling the perfect kicking action in your imagination, and at the same time affirming to yourself that you're performing it as smoothly as silk, can bring about only one result: you develop a kicking action as smooth as silk.

As we learned in the previous chapter, it takes about a month for an affirmation to bed itself into your subconscious, so that it automatically produces the desired reaction to a given set of circumstances. Employing visualisation alongside affirmation won't necessarily speed the process up—our experience suggests Napoleon has his own in-built timetable for accepting new imprints on the subconscious—but it will definitely bed the desired reaction in place more permanently and firmly. It's like the difference between writing 'Mum' on your shoulder with a felt pen (spoken affirmations alone), and getting a tattoo artist to do it (affirmations and visualisation combined).

To the legion of kickers who model themselves on him, Grant Fox holds the patent on the classic, perfect kicking action. Can't you just picture him slotting those penalties and conversions with that silken, breezy technique? So, if you aspire to kick as he does, put yourself in his picture. See yourself in your mind's eye, in your imagination, stroking the ball 'as smooth as silk'. Don't just imagine —see.

See with your mind's eye that oiled Fox action—only it's you in the picture: your face, your shape. It's you feeling that ball leaving your instep. If you're a fly half, see yourself performing all those other skills that Fox mastered and which the position demands. Whatever position you play in, see in your mind's eye your most admired player in action, then put yourself in the picture. See yourself as the great Australian lock John Eales scaling the heights to take a line-out ball, or All Black flanker Josh Kronfeld scything someone down in a tackle, or Jonah Lomu, ball in hand, attacking a would-be tackler.

With practice you quickly become fluent in the mental language of forming clear, precise pictures—videos in the imagination—of what your affirmation is saying. The greater your fluency, the quicker the dream will become reality.

What you're doing is describing to Siggy what you want to see happen, by supplying him with clear, vibrant pictures of your goal achieved. Once he's got the picture, and has it stored away as a file on his hard disk, Siggy is set to exploit any opportunity of making the goal a reality. And at that point you start playing rugby the way you previously only imagined you could.

The same affirmation-to-achievement process can be applied equally to specific and, especially, time-oriented goals—such as reaching a particular level in the game in a particular year. See yourself playing the big match, much as a spectator would see you. See the positive signals you're giving off to your opponents. See how you've improved so dramatically over the years that the selectors can't overlook you. See how cool, calm, relaxed and confident you look as you take the field for your World Cup final. The goal is to make that picture so clear, so precise and believable, that you accept it as real. And that's when it starts to become real.

It's a matter of belief. It's not the blind belief of the religious or political fundamentalist. Instead, it's an informed belief based on the huge database on Siggy's hard disk that comprises our knowledge of ourselves—a database created by ourselves, for ourselves.

Henry Ford, the man whose Model T brought motoring to the masses and untold wealth to his family, once said: 'You can have anything you can imagine yourself as having.' Another way of putting it is: You are what you believe you are. What Ford was talking about was the extraordinary power of creative visualisation. Marry this power up to the goal-setting and affirmation programmes, and you've started a sequence of changes in attitude that guarantees success.

You see the goal, you believe the goal, you achieve the goal.

Here's all it takes to organise your affirmation-visualisation sessions. Get away somewhere by yourself, either in a comfy chair or stretched out on the bed. Start off by stating your affirmation out loud, with your eyes open. (The trick in this is to prime Siggy for the session by also sending him a signal through one of the physical senses—in this case hearing. Reading the affirmation off a card adds another sense—sight. If you could touch, smell or taste your affirmation as well, so much the better.) Now close your eyes and run through the movie that visualises the affirmation. That's all. Do it twice a day. You don't have to spend more than five minutes each session on it, and the results will astound you.

Don't just apply it to ultimate goals. Try it on successive medium-term intermediate goals. When the ultimate goal starts to loom on your horizon of achievements, then switch to the movie of your ultimate achievement and play it over in your mind repeatedly until your own great day when informed imagination and clarity of purpose finally bridge the gulf between goal and reality.

Play-by-play use of creative visualisation

Of course Grant Fox isn't the only sporting great who can attest to the effectiveness of creative visualisation in achieving goals. Perhaps the most famous proponent of the technique was the Golden Bear, Jack Nicklaus, still one of the best golfers ever. In his books on coaching Nicklaus says that, before he swings the club, he forms a picture in his mind of the shot he's going to play. The picture is vibrant and he packs it with as much detail as he can assimilate: the weather, the colour of the sky, the shapes of the trees. When playing an iron to the green, he takes his stance, then pictures the ball rising into the sky, hovering over the green, then coming down and landing next to the pin. The clearer and more precise the picture is, the better he knows the shot will be.

Nicklaus uses pictures to have his Napoleon communicate to his Siggy the result he wants Siggy to achieve. If he communicates precisely enough, he knows he can rely on his Siggy to duplicate the mental movie. Nicklaus has, in effect, already played the shot before he swings the club.

Of course rugby works to a vastly different—and much more pressured—timetable than does golf: the rugby player doesn't have the luxury of a quiet stroll to the ball during which he can visualise what he's going to do next. More importantly, the rugby player faces a whole range of options when play resumes. The golfer simply has to select his target (the fairway or the pin) and go for it. But, outside of set plays, the rugby player usually has only a broad idea which of a range of skill options he'll be required to exercise when play resumes. The golfer has one option, the rugby player a range of them.

But despite the differences in time-scale and the number of playing options to choose from, the principles of creative visualisation apply to rugby in exactly the same way as they do to golf or any other sport you care to name. There's enough time during those lulls in the rugby match—after Napoleon has absorbed all that pure and uncluttered data and passed it on to Siggy—to do a quick visualising review not just of the options available to you when the game resumes, but of you exercising each of those options. The pass, the tackle, the kick, the line-out jump, the scrum heave, whatever—it takes just a couple of seconds to run through each of your stored videos of yourself in action (perhaps modelled on your favourite player) exercising each of the options or demands you'll encounter when play resumes.

Don't close your eyes during this play-by-play visualisation exercise. Instead, exercise your imagination alongside your physical sense of sight. If you're a fly half and your options include a wipers kick, 'see' the ball in real life sail in behind the opposing backline, smack between the winger and the fullback. If you're a lock forward, 'see' the ball sail into your hands from the line-out throw. If you're a fullback and you're expecting the opposition fly half to drop a bomb on you, 'see' that ball arc through the air and land safely in your arms.

The effect of this exercise is two-fold. Firstly, it gives Siggy an early indication as to which of the practised skill files he's about to have to recover from his database and put into action. If Siggy's got those skill files at his fingertips he's going to be that fraction of a second faster in selecting and acting upon the most appropriate option. And, in selecting options in the heat of a rugby game, those fractions of a second count. They can make the difference between a good response to a given situation and an inspired one, between a predictable response and one that takes the opposition by surprise, between sneaking across the line for a try and being pulled up short.

The rugby player doesn't have the benefit of those five-minute breaks between plays that golfers enjoy, but there's nothing stopping him from compressing exactly the same mental exercises into the 10- or 20-second pauses that he encounters throughout a game.

The second benefit this exercise offers is that in order to do it, you have to switch Napoleon off after he's done his quick stint of practising awareness and feeding the pure data into Siggy. Napoleon's activities are reduced to the strictly useful. He becomes almost as much a tool, a machine, as Siggy, because Napoleon is left with no time to waste on fear of failure or fear of getting hurt.

While you're developing the skills of positive visualisation, keep an eye out for examples of negative visualisation by other players during games. There are a couple of classic situations where the downside of an overactive or unrestrained Napoleon can be seen on the rugby field: waiting under a high kick, and taking a drop goal from the field. In both these situations the player is temporarily isolated from every other player on the paddock and reduced entirely to his own resources.

The high kick is the first test that a team routinely makes of the opposing fullback. The up-and-under asks the crude question, 'How do you like waiting there under the ball knowing that opposing players are charging down on you with the intention of flattening you the moment you get your hands on it?' It's moments like these that test the relationship between Napoleon and Siggy. What tends to happen is that, instead of leaving Siggy to perform the simple take of the high ball that he's achieved a thousand times in practice, and for which Siggy has plenty of skill files stored on his hard disk, Napoleon interferes by feeding in the entirely useless knowledge that half the opposing team is bearing down with malevolent intent. Confused by this irrelevant information, Siggy fluffs the catch—and the opposition backs and loosies rub their hands with glee. What the fullback needed to do was screen out the extra information, the negative visualisation of himself being creamed, thereby leaving Siggy to exercise the fairly basic skill of catching the high ball. The stuff that Napoleon fed him about opposing players is entirely useless, because there's nothing Siggy can do about them until after he's taken the catch. The educated Napoleon ignores the approaching opposing players, and feeds Siggy only the relevant information—the ball's height and trajectory, and its estimated time of arrival in his arms.

Similarly, you'll see negative visualisation at work in attempts at drop goals. On the face of it, a drop goal is the easiest way of all to score points: all you've got to do is get up to the opponents' end of the paddock and kick the ball through the posts from right in front.

So how come the overwhelming majority of attempts miss? It's because the kicker has created the negative mind-picture of opposing loose forwards charging the kick down if he doesn't get it away quickly enough. So he rushes his strike—and fluffs the kick. Yet the information about the opposing loosies is irrelevant to Siggy. Siggy's skill files have more than enough data on drop-kicking to secure the three easy points, but if Napoleon also tosses in the information about approaching loosies, Siggy thinks this has to be taken into account too—and there's nothing in his files about both drop-kicking and rushing to avoid the loosies.

The positive way to visualise both the high-kick take and the drop-kick goal is with an awareness of the likely approach of opposing players, but a prior acknowledgement of their irrelevance to the exercise. Visualise yourself standing under the high ball, aware of where other players are (so you know what to do once you've secured the ball), but see and feel yourself consciously excluding that information until Siggy has exercised the necessary catching skills. Similarly with the drop kick: see yourself executing it unhurriedly despite the opposing loosies and inside backs buzzing about you.

Connect your positive visualisation with positive affirmations—'I have a kicking (or catching) action that's as smooth as silk, and I always have plenty of time to perform it without interference from other players'—and watch how steady you become under the high ball, see how big a percentage of your dropped-goal attempts succeed.

We'll cover the technical aspects of Grant Fox's kicking in a later chapter, but now we need to look at creating the most receptive condition of the mind for creative visualisation both on and off the field. The most receptive mind is the relaxed one and, like all the mind-training concepts we introduce in this book, relaxation is just a matter of technique, of knowing how to relax.

—9—
Relaxation techniques

> My special place. It's a place no amount of hurt or danger can deface. I put things back together there. It all falls right in place. —JONI MITCHELL

Different sports need different styles of pre-game preparation: a rugby player's preparation is not the same as, say, a lawn bowler's. Lawn bowls requires only minimal physical input. To be effective that input has to be subtle and gentle rather than explosive and aggressive. The lawn bowler's muscles have to be relaxed, tension has to be dissipated, and the delivery of the bowl has to be smooth, flowing and controlled.

The rugby player, by contrast, has to get his adrenalin flowing, triggering the fight part of his fight-or-flight syndrome. He flexes his muscles, pumps up, and prepares to throw himself at the opposition: he's all primed energy and targeted aggression. But, just like the lawn bowler, the rugby player needs an inner calm to override all the external stimuli. There's no contradiction in that either: the rugby player taking the field needs to be in an altered physical state, with both his pulse and his body temperature cranked up well above normal (and preferably with a knot in his stomach from the pre-game nerves). But at the same time his mind should be operating in a cool and clinical atmosphere of its own.

Rugby, like most contact sports, comprises a succession of explosive outputs requiring stamina, strength and physical commitment, followed by brief recovery periods. We mention lawn bowls in the same context because, as noted in the introduction to this book, that was the sport in which Mark de Lacy pioneered these techniques of mind-training for sportspeople and Peter Belliss proved them. The principles are the same for bowls as for rugby—indeed, as for virtually any endeavour in life. What the *Think & Play* series does is apply those principles to the demands of different sports in a practical and user-friendly way.

You could hardly find two sports less alike than bowls and rugby, but what players of both codes have in common is that they play their best under the influence of that inner calm that arises from quiet confidence. Surprised that two such utterly different sports should require the same mindset? Don't be. If there were some empirical way of comparing Grant Fox's state of mind as he helped New Zealand win the inaugural Rugby World Cup of 1987, and Peter Belliss's on his way to one of his world lawn bowls titles, there'd be little to distinguish between the two. The physical demands of both sports are as different as they could be, but the mental attitudes of these respective world champions are interchangeable.

Later in this book we'll devote a whole chapter to Fox's famously effective kicking techniques and the mental training exercises that produced them, but first let's look at the concept of relaxation, and its importance to the working relationship between Siggy and Napoleon.

Just as it is vital to practise individual skills and team coordination, so too is it vital to practise relaxing under the pressure of competition. Hours a week spent polishing our skills and teamwork is a waste of time if we tense up under the pressure of a tight game. We'd be better off spending half the time on physical practice and the rest on practising relaxation.

And, yes, 'practising' is the operative word. Relaxation is not a matter of doing nothing else, of sitting on our bums watching television, or scoffing a few pints at the pub. Those things might, in fact, be quite stressful. True relaxation is an exercise, as deliberate and performance-oriented as practising with the team.

Relaxation is learned behaviour. It doesn't necessarily come naturally, and for people who work in high-pressure occupations—such as policing, nursing and parenting—genuine relaxation can be a challenging but essential skill to master.

Yet the ability to stay relaxed throughout the game is crucial to the rugby player. It's important to be able to relax before a game;

it's just as important to be able to relax during and after it. Given the immense energy and commitment that rugby demands, you could be forgiven for thinking there's no room for relaxation while you're playing. And in purely physical terms, you'd be right: your body can never relax completely during a game of rugby. But, if you are to fully realise your potential as a rugby player, your mind—also known as our friend Napoleon—must remain relaxed throughout the game, even when it's practising awareness during the gaps in the action.

So, for on-the-field mental relaxation, you practise relaxation off the field. And if you can tie your relaxation exercises into your off-field affirmation and visualisation ones, you're creating the optimum environment for developing all these mental skills.

Indeed, it's fair to say that you visualise and make affirmations most effectively if your body is relaxed and your mind is quiet and uncluttered so it can absorb mental pictures without distraction. Physical relaxation might be easier to achieve on a sofa in your living room than on the pitch in the middle of a rugby match, but keep in mind that your body also has to use those gaps in play to recover from its previous exertions. And the body recovers fastest when it's most relaxed.

So learning to relax both on and off the field is vital to improving our game. Continuous practice of a relaxation technique results in two useful psychological changes. The first is muscular, the second is to do with brain-wave patterns.

Muscular control

The key to controlling the muscular tension that builds up before and during a game is breathing.

Our pattern of breathing changes with our emotional state. If we're angry, our breathing accelerates to shallow inhalations and short, sharp exhalations. If we're sad or sobbing, inhaling is fitful and jerky, while exhaling is weak. Tiredness makes us yawn; fear makes us hold our breath. So it follows that, since breathing patterns reflect our emotional state, changing our breathing can change the way we feel.

As physical tiredness catches up with you during a game, deep, relaxed breathing will accelerate your recovery (and, incidentally, make you feel less tired than you actually are). You need to relax mentally to exercise awareness during the pauses in the game, and you need to relax physically to speed up your recovery. Proper breathing, as a conscious exercise, will help you with both.

The way to breathe properly is through the diaphragm. Normal breathing is shallow, and it tends to be especially so when you're trying to repay the oxygen debt that comes from hard physical exercise. Diaphragm breathing involves getting the lungs to fill from the bottom up. You feel the lower rib cage expand first, then the chest, until the lungs are filled to capacity. 'Suck that air in,' the captain tells you as you try to get your breath during a game. That's right: suck it in from the bottom of your lungs up. Cram in as much air as you can, so your lungs can grab all the oxygen out of it, and your heart can pump it through the bloodstream to where the oxygen debt is greatest (usually in your legs). Feel your belly draw down and out until you can inhale no more. Then expel all the air quickly through the mouth until your lungs are empty. As you breathe out, as the belly draws up and in, feel—that is, make yourself aware of—all the tension floating out with the air. Then suck in the next lungful.

In your off-the-field relaxation breathing, to prepare for or to accompany your affirmation and visualisation exercises, you can breathe more slowly and deliberately than when you're trying to make up oxygen debt during a game. Again, be conscious of filling your lungs from the bottom up. Breathe in through your nose (which you can't do so well under heavy oxygen debt) and out through your mouth—slowly, slowly. When your breathing has settled into a slow pattern, and you're stretched out comfortably in a chair or on a bed, then you can start the affirmations and visualisations.

These days this sort of breathing is also employed on the field (once the oxygen debt has been repaid) by goal-kickers. Indeed, Grant Fox, more than any other New Zealand player, made deep aerobic breathing (as distinct from anaerobic breathing, which is what you do when you're in oxygen debt) a standard practice among goal-kickers. Fox went through a little routine that varies for each player, but remains exactly the same from one kick to the next.

It usually involves sucking air in through the nose, then exhaling completely. Some kickers give a little waggle of the fingers, as Fox did, or let their shoulders slump at the end of the exhalation. Most of them then repeat the exercise two or three times, during which they mentally rehearse their kicking action, and visualise the path the ball will take between the posts. Their hearts may still be working at over a hundred beats to the minute—half as much again as those of the spectators watching them—but their bodies and minds are relaxed, their Napoleons aware, and their Siggys primed. Then they switch Napoleon off, and turn the job over to Siggy: they move in to kick.

Here's an exercise to show you how important relaxation of the muscles can be for the kicker. Find two small objects of different weight—say, an apple and an orange. Tense the muscles in your arm and hand and pick up the objects one after the other, making sure you grasp them firmly. See if you can tell the difference in weight.

Now repeat the exercise, but this time first do the aerobic diaphragm-breathing exercise described earlier. As you breathe out, imagine all the tension flowing down your arm and out of your hands through your fingertips, until you're completely relaxed. Now pick up each object gently and sense the difference in weight.

Notice the difference? Moral of the story: you'll find it a lot easier to judge kicking weight and distance when your muscles are free from tension.

This is a core principle for anyone involved in an exercise, such as kicking, where skill is more important than the purely physical component. Tension in the muscles distorts the information being sent to Siggy. The relaxed kicker can trust Siggy to add, say, that fraction of weight to a kick that's at the extreme end of his range without pulling or slicing it. The uptight kicker tries to add the weight but, since trying necessarily involves tension, he's not giving Siggy a fair go at making the necessary adjustment from short range to long range.

Brain-wave control

Earlier we discussed the ease with which young children learn such complex skills as walking and talking. Science has shown that brain-wave rhythms are much slower in the toddler than in the adult. As we grow older, these rhythms accelerate rapidly because our sensory capacity is expanding to take in an ever-increasing range of sights, sounds and smells. Adults tend to lose the ability to concentrate on a single event or to learn quickly from it—the way a child does— and it's apparent that the change in brain-wave rhythm from slow to fast is responsible.

The child operates at what the specialists call alpha level, which comprises 8 to 13 brain-wave cycles a second. The adult is at beta level, which varies from 14 to 40 cycles a second. Excitement, tension and fear cause brain waves to speed up even further. The slower the brain-wave rhythm, the better we concentrate.

A baby can focus on one activity to the exclusion of everything else, and it's this level of concentration that lets it learn so rapidly. As the maturing child begins to be affected by the sensory bombardment of modern living, brain waves move from alpha to beta rhythm, and its ability to concentrate diminishes.

It's a bit like the reception on a television set: with just one signal coming through, the picture is clear and detailed. Multiply the signals and we begin to get ghosting and interference. The picture becomes fuzzy and scrambled because the set can't isolate one message from the many its aerial is picking up.

We can learn a lot from watching babies concentrate. The main lesson is that we all once had this ability—and we can get it back.

The way to recover it is to learn how to slow brain-wave patterns down to alpha levels, and this is where relaxation techniques come into play. Constant practice in relaxation will improve our ability to concentrate and make affirmation and visualisation more effective. Relaxation lets us clear out the interference and stress caused by sensory bombardment, so our minds can absorb, without distraction, pictures of our goals. As a bonus, you'll find practising one of the following techniques will lower your blood pressure and eliminate stress—it's like having an annual holiday twice a day.

There are many choices open to the competitor who wants to create a favourable mental environment. Hypnosis—either self-, or induced by a clinical hypnotist—is one. Other techniques used by successful sportspeople are: breathing meditation; transcendental meditation; and autogenic training.

Breathing meditation

This expands the concept of diaphragm breathing described earlier. As in all relaxation techniques, you should practise it in a place where you'll be undisturbed for twenty minutes. The best times to do it are on getting up in the morning, and before the evening meal.

Sit in a comfortable chair with both feet on the floor, your back straight and your hands resting palm-up on your lap. Do the deep-breathing exercise (described earlier) three times, visualising as you exhale all the tension flowing out of your body through your fingertips.

Now concentrate on your breathing. Follow the air in through your nose—feeling it fill your tummy, then your chest—and out, sensing the air travelling through your chest, throat and mouth. Don't try to change the rhythm of your breathing: just be aware of the flow.

If other thoughts drift into your head, don't fight them but, when you realise they're there, gently switch your attention back to the breathing. In, out; in, out.

As you become more and more relaxed you'll feel a warmth spread through your body and often a tingling sensation in your fingers and toes. After fifteen minutes you'll feel wonderfully relaxed and you can then spend the next five minutes visualising your affirmations.

You'll find this exercise most refreshing: twenty minutes and you'll feel like you've had a whole night's sleep.

Transcendental meditation

It isn't possible to teach this technique in a book. Like the associated practice of yoga, it has to be taught individually by a trained teacher. It's not within the scope of this book to explain how the technique works, but there are some misconceptions about it that should be cleared up, because more and more sportspeople are employing it.

Transcendental meditation involves the repetition of a sound—called a mantra, and given to you by the teacher—made or spoken under the breath. The sound is simple and has no meaning or significance to the meditator, but concentrating on it eventually takes the mind to an altered state of consciousness, pure awareness, where brain-wave patterns and breathing slow down and you enter a state of blissful relaxation.

It sounds wonderful, and it is. You remain wide awake and totally aware of your surroundings, yet without thought.

It is Siggy and Napoleon's nature to prefer the more pleasurable of two alternatives. For example, if you were reading and your favourite song came on the radio, your attention would switch to the music, because effortless listening is more pleasurable than the effort of reading. By concentrating on the mantra or meaningless sound, your mind gradually switches off, of its own accord, to the more pleasurable state of consciousness we used to experience as children.

It's in this state that we can most effectively transmit positive ideas to our subconscious. Apart from the dissolving of stress, the advantage of TM is that it doesn't matter how sceptical you are about it: believe it or not, it works. It seems to work especially well for sceptics.

The main misconceptions about TM are that it's a belief system, or a religion. It's neither. It's a technique that's practised by people in every country, from all walks of life and with widely differing religions—or none at all. The effects are cumulative: the more you practise TM, the less stress you feel.

Meditation, as a technique to prepare for sport, induces an awareness or alpha state where Siggy is at his most receptive for his regular dose of affirmation and visualisation. It's like recharging the batteries of an appliance: it not only helps to improve your concentration on the sports field, but contributes to living stress-free in what has become a pressure-cooker society.

Autogenic training

This is an exercise you do twice daily in twenty-minute spells. Ask someone to read the instructions out to you, or record them and play them back until you've memorised the steps and can repeat them silently to yourself.

Lie down on a bed or on the floor, on your back with a firm pillow supporting your head. Your clothing should be loose. Breathe through the diaphragm and imagine—feel—the weight of your body pushing down on the mattress or carpet. Imagine—feel—the bed or floor pushing up as you push down.

Shift your awareness to your feet, and imagine them warm and heavy. Feel the skin and bones getting heavier and warmer, heavier and warmer.

Now the heat and weight start to spread up your legs to your calf muscles. Feel your calves heavy and warm.

Now your knees feel heavy and warm, and the sensation is spreading into your thigh muscles and buttocks. Heavy and warm.

The heat moves into your tummy and travels up into your chest. Your muscles and bones feel heavy and warm, with a pleasant tingling sensation. Feel this sensation in your lower back as it gets heavier and warmer.

Feel the heaviness and warmth move up your spine and into your shoulders and neck. The muscles around your upper back relax with the pleasant heat. Feel tension disappear as the weight and the heat consume your body.

Imagine all the tension travelling up your spine and into your shoulders—then down your arms, exiting your body through your fingertips. The place where the tension was is now twice as heavy, twice as warm. Your body is heavy and warm.

Now feel the weight and heat enter your head. Neck, throat, chin, cheeks—heavy and warm, heavy and warm. Mouth and jaw—relaxed and tension-free. Heavy and warm. Nose, ears, scalp—all becoming heavy and warm. Your whole body heavy and warm.

Feel a cool breeze start to fan your forehead. Your forehead becomes cooler and cooler. The rest of your body is heavy and warm.

Now your whole body is deeply relaxed. Your skin tingles as healing energy flows through it, revitalising your system. Imagine yourself floating on warm, fluffy clouds—you are rising as you breathe in—sinking down into their warmth as you breathe out.

Feel how calm and peaceful you are. Imagine feeling this way when you're playing rugby. Relaxed, calm—even graceful.

Know that you can enter this state whenever you like.

Now take three deep breaths. Feel energy flow in as you inhale, and tension leave as you exhale.

Open your eyes and sit up. Pretend you're a cat stretching after a sleep.

There—now you're ready for anything.

When you first start these exercises you may feel a bit awkward or self-conscious, but that'll pass quickly as you see the benefits flow in.

Once you're comfortable with one of these techniques you'll find you're in company with an army of top athletes who swear by them—company that represents an extraordinary variety of sports, from Kenyan marathon runner Douglas Wakahuri to Olympic windsurfing gold medallist Bruce Kendall.

All the techniques described so far—goal-setting, affirmation, creative visualisation and relaxation—are there to use if you want to improve both your game and your attitude to it. Not only will you begin to experience unprecedented success, but, perhaps more importantly, you'll enjoy the sport more.

These systems are designed to produce your peak experience—the one that reveals to you what your potential really is, the benchmark by which you rate all future performances.

–10–
Anchoring

> Be outrageous! People who achieve mastery have the ability to be outrageous. GITA BELLIN

The mood we wake up in on any given morning tends to dominate the way we operate for the rest of the day. If we start off in a bad mood, it's likely that everything we do will reinforce that negative start. Bad temper seems to create bad luck, arguments and disagreements—even aches and pains. What we need to realise is that each experience during the day at work, at home or on the sporting field, is simply an experience. But it's our mood or overall attitude that dictates the significance of that experience to us.

Let's create two characters, Joe Moody and Jill Happy, who don't know each other but are destined to meet later in the day.

Joe has woken up in a foul mood intensified by the kids being late for school, a breakfast that tasted like cardboard and his wife complaining of a headache.

Jill is a happy, positive person who meditates and lives a stress-free life. When Jill woke up that morning her husband was complaining of a headache. Jill told him to rest while she got him a cup of tea and an aspirin. The kids were running late for school, so she set goals for them to complete preparations in record time. The children responded and made it to school before the bell.

On the way to work, Joe and Jill meet unexpectedly at an intersection. Joe is still fuming over his lousy breakfast, fails to give way, and hits Jill's car amidships. Joe is clearly in the wrong and both cars suffer minor damage, but no one is hurt.

Arriving at work, Joe looks flushed and angry, and tells his workmates, 'I don't believe how unlucky I've been this morning. The wife's never stopped complaining, the kids were late for school and, to top it off, some lunatic woman driver pranged my car. It'll cost me a fortune. I just know what the rest of the day will be like.' Then he stomps into his office, slamming the door behind him.

Jill, on the other hand, arrives at work beaming, greets her workmates warmly, asks how they feel, then tells them, 'I don't believe how lucky I've been this morning. Some poor bloke who'd had a rough morning didn't see me at an intersection and hit my car. I could've been killed, but instead all that happened was a couple of dented panels. I just know I'm going to have a great day.' She smiles and happily goes off to her office.

The one thing that Joe and Jill had in common, the accident, was simply an experience. All experiences get lost in the mists of time. It's how we look at them that matters. We can choose to look at them in a positive or a negative way. People like Jill exist. They've learned to control their thought patterns and attitudes to the extent that they look for something positive in every experience. As a result, they are happy, balanced people who love life and live in harmony with their environment and themselves. As another result, good things seem to come their way.

The most important point to take from this little drama is that we can control how we feel about an experience, whether it's a car accident or a game of rugby—and we can do it in advance.

Many of us seem to have been conditioned to react to most things negatively at least half the time but, by using the techniques outlined here, we can begin to reverse this conditioning.

By using a technique called anchoring, we can arrest negative reactions to given experiences and replace them with positive ones. You can use the technique to change from a losing mode (Napoleon trying to convince you that you're playing badly, and that you should try to exert more control over Siggy to turn things round), into peak experience mode (where Napoleon shuts up and hands over the reins to Siggy, and you know you're giving yourself the best possible chance of playing to your potential). You're not worried about losing because you know the game is just an experience. Consequently, you enjoy yourself.

The technique of anchoring has to be put in place when you're deeply relaxed. Visualisation is central to it, and the more practised you are at forming mental pictures the better it works.

You have to put your anchors in place—like tools in the toolbox of your car—before you need them. Then you just pluck them out whenever circumstances call for them. Here's how you create your toolbox of anchors:

1. Go through your relaxation programme so that you feel relaxed, warm and peaceful. The best system to use to get there is a breathing exercise. Breathe in through your nose for a count of eight. Hold your breath for a count of ten. Breathe out through your mouth for a count of twelve. Concentrate on the timing until you can do it without counting, and remember to breathe through your diaphragm, from the bottom up.
2. Turn on a make-believe television set and form a picture of yourself, tense and negative during a rugby match. See yourself frowning, complaining, unlucky, playing poorly and in losing mode. When you see clearly what you look and feel like, decide that you don't want that look and feeling any more. Then pick up an imaginary pot of paint and hurl it at the screen, so that the paint obliterates the picture.
3. Watch as the paint runs down the screen, dissolving the picture as it goes. Say to yourself as you watch the negative picture disintegrate, 'I don't want that feeling any more. I don't need that feeling any more. There, it's gone.'
4. Now go back to your blank screen and visualise yourself in peak experience mode. See yourself relaxed and confident, with an unshakeably high expectation of success. Relive a time when you felt on top of the world, when you had that Midas touch, were playing like a wizard and could do no wrong. Remember how you felt, and picture yourself as others would have seen you.
5. When the memory and visualisation become clear (you may find yourself smiling), form your fist into a trademark grip—one that you want to be special to you. It could be with your thumb between your first two fingers—anything, as long as you can remember it and repeat it at will.

6. When your picture is vibrant, strong and totally positive, make a vigorous gesture—a punch, say, or a hammering in the air—with your special fist-grip. And say out loud, 'Yeah!'

7. Now wipe the entire picture out, and repeat all the steps from 2 to 6.

If you practise this technique twice a day for at least three weeks, Napoleon will begin to recognise the gesture of the special fist, the punching and saying 'Yeah!', as a signal to switch into positive mode. His reactions to it will have been preprogrammed.

If you feel tense and negative during a game, and things seem to be slipping away, make the fist and its accompanying gesture, say 'Yeah!' and you'll generate an immediate mood swing.

You can use this method in all sorts of circumstances, creating a new signal for any mood or feeling you want to re-create. That's what anchoring is.

When you have a crucial role to play in a game, and you want to give yourself the best possible chance of rising to the occasion, you can use anchoring to duplicate those earlier times when you performed particularly well under pressure. You're able to recall instantly and vividly how you felt—the intensity of concentration and the huge feeling of satisfaction that that earlier performance gave you. The signal and sound trigger the response you want. Napoleon will remember to associate the movement and sound with the feeling generated by that earlier performance, and can replicate the mood—the mode—that produced it.

The supercharger

Within the context of anchoring, we've developed a technique especially for forwards who suddenly find themselves with the ball in hand and a goodly proportion of the opposition pack directly in their path, or any player given a couple of metres in which to line up a tackle. We call it the supercharger, and it's geared to produce either the 'big hit' tackle, or an effective straight-ahead ball-in-hand charge where there's no real expectation of breaking through, only of developing that essential go-forward by hitting your opponents with every ounce of power and aggression in your being.

ABOVE: Grant Fox's successor in the place-kicking role for the All Blacks is Canterbury's Andrew Mehrtens, another of the game's notable thinkers.

RIGHT: Visualisation in practice: South Africa's Joel Stransky in the last seconds before he moves in to execute a place-kick. He is 'seeing' the ball sail between the uprights even before he has kicked it. Visualisation is rehearsal, and the more detailed the rehearsal the better the execution.

Australia's Matt Burke demonstrates Grant Fox's contention that the placement of the non-kicking foot is central to accurate place-kicking.

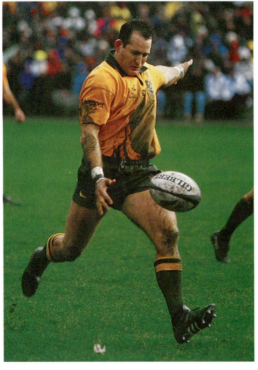

Master punter David Campese of Australia prepares to let fly. As with place-kicking, accurate punting is dependent on the quality of the skill-files scored on Siggy, your personal inbuilt computer.

No computer can remotely approximate the speed and complexity of your personal inbuilt Siggy in co-ordinating the myriad internal and external variables involved in accurate place-kicking. The kicker here is All Black Andrew Mehrtens.

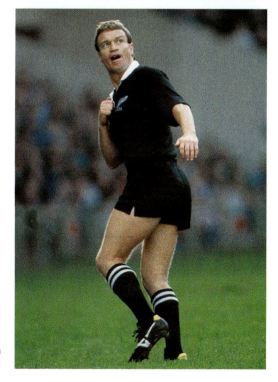

The place-kicking exercise over, the relevant skill-file can be set aside until the next time it's needed. Positive reinforcement is the ultimate vindication of affirmation and visualisation exercises—in this case, 'Well done, Siggy' is written all over Grant Fox's face.

Siggy has only a tiny fraction of a second in which to select and activate the most appropriate skill-file for the circumstances. Taken in a tackle, Australian centre Tim Horan presents the ball perfectly for his forwards against South Africa.

The apparently simple act of scooping up a bobbling ball involves an extraordinarily complex coordination of muscular reactions to instantly updated visual information. Here South African fullback Percy Montgomery performs under the watchful eye of Breyton Paulse as the All Blacks' Tana Umaga looms.

The supercharger is sudden, explosive, short-term stuff—it lasts no more than a couple of seconds—and its intention is simply to maximise your impact. It concentrates all your power and aggression in a short eruption of energy. Because it's so expensive in terms of energy usage, you wouldn't unleash it more than half a dozen times a game. If you tried to play the whole game under its influence, you wouldn't last five minutes, but it's a potentially lethal weapon in your bag of psycho-tricks.

The way it works is that the instant you get the ball, or you perceive a big-hit tackle opportunity, you yell (or just grunt, if you don't like making too much noise) and make your first step forward a ferocious stamp into the ground. Bang that foot down, let out your yell or grunt, and fling yourself at the opponent(s). The yell and the stamp are the triggers that tell Siggy to let all the dogs off the leash for that brief charge, and you use the anchoring techniques described above to preprogramme your Siggy for it.

Note that there's no subtlety in the supercharge. You're just plain exploding at and into the opposition like a gun going off. Technique is less important than the psychological effect on your opponent(s) of your explosive impact.

Alongside goal-setting, affirmation, visualisation and relaxation, anchoring—and the short, sharp supercharge that is a form of anchoring—is a potent weapon to have in your mental arsenal.

−11−
Peak experiences

> We should be careful to get out of an experience only the wisdom that is in it—and stop there, lest we be like the cat that sits down on a hot stove lid. She will never sit down on a hot stove lid again—and that is well; but also she will never sit down on a cold one any more.
> MARK TWAIN

At some time in their careers most sportspeople experience what athletes call a peak experience. It's a magical sensation: you feel as though you can do anything. On the rugby field you feel ten feet tall, unstoppable, indestructible.

Peak experiences typically happen out of the blue. You can't figure out what precipitated one, or why, and you're left with a sense of wonder at the way you played and at the confidence you felt.

There are millions of examples of supposedly average rugby players who, for some unaccountable reason, suddenly start playing well above themselves during a match, flinging themselves around the pitch, tackling like demons, running like panthers, handling the ball as if they've got glue on their fingers, rucking and scrummaging like bulldozers. After the match their team-mates ask incredulously, 'What got into you? You were a whirlwind out there.' This phenomenon is the peak experience.

Runners will tell you that in a peak experience they feel more like they're floating than running, golfers make jokes of their own handicaps, darts players just can't miss that triple 20. It happens in all sports, and psychologists have isolated eight components which seem to be common to all peak experiences. They are:

1. Mental quiet

This is often the aspect of the peak experience that sportspeople remember most fondly. You're overwhelmed by a sense of inner peace and tranquillity, no matter how hectic the pace of the game. Time seems to have slowed down, allowing you to concentrate fully. You cease to be aware of distractions—such as the noise or silence of spectators—or any stimuli irrelevant to the sporting task in hand.

2. Physical relaxation

There is no tension. Muscles relax and take on heightened tonal and sensory qualities even during periods of the most intense activity.

3. 'In the now'

Mind and body come together in perfect unison. You play automatically and effortlessly, and without conscious thought. Whatever happened before or may happen later, good or bad, is unimportant, inconsequential. All your energy is focused on this game, this moment.

4. Confidence and optimism

You are pervaded by confidence, whatever the match situation. You look forward to the opposition playing superbly so you can show how much better you are.

5. Energy

You enjoy a feeling of extraordinary well-being. You are fit, happy, and have power and control over events.

6. Awareness

You are tuned in to your environment, open only to influences helpful to your game. Sensory information is accurate and focused on selecting the most useful and relevant data from among the deluge of messages from your highly tuned senses. Frequently, the competitor in a peak experience becomes capable of predicting accurately what the opponent will do next: a fly half knows instinctively what his opposite number intends doing when in possession.

7. Control
You know, without conscious thought, what to do and how to do it. Results occur exactly as you intend them to.

8. 'In a cocoon'
You feel as though you're perfectly safe behind a barrier that excludes all worry, doubt and fear. Negative thoughts don't enter the mind. You concentrate fully, insulated against extraneous data.

If you've had these eight sensations at the same time, you've had a 'peak experience'. The nearest thing to it in other facets of life is the experience of falling in love: the feelings are hard to describe because they're so intensely personal and individual, but you certainly know when it has hit you. And if you have to ask what it's like, it hasn't happened to you yet.

Another thing about peak experiences is that they seem to come when the athlete has a particularly strong expectation of success—and there's usually a trigger that sets them off. The trigger for a rugby player might be as simple as a positive word in his ear from the coach, which starts a chain of thought that rapidly deduces that, 'This is my day—I am invincible—everything I do turns to gold.' The eight components of the peak experience begin to manifest themselves, generating an 'I can't lose' conviction. You start to play 'in the now', and get on a high so memorable it may be enough to keep you playing the game season after season solely in the hope of experiencing it again.

But while the high is fun, much of its potential to encourage and motivate you in the future depends on how you deal with it immediately after it happens. The most important rule is this: don't spew out a heap of negative affirmations the moment you're back in the clubhouse. Don't be amazed by what you've done. Don't say, 'I don't believe how well I played', or 'I was incredibly lucky'—that would be suggesting that what happened wasn't real. Don't let yourself presume that your normal performance is real, and that what you've just done was a fluke. That would waste the opportunity that a peak experience presents.

Look at it in a realistic light: the peak experience is a phenomenon generated by an abnormal expectation of success. It's the expectation that's abnormal, not the experience. Make the heightened expectation normal, and your normal game rises to the quality it attained during your peak experience.

A peak experience is caused by a high expectation of success. Having this expectation removes fear and negativity from the nervous system, allowing performance to equal potential. To repeat the performance then, you have to cultivate an equally high expectation of success.

Top athletes in all sports draw confidence from their peak experiences. They know them as clear and unmistakable signs of their potential. Among the techniques proven to assist sportspeople in creating that expectation of success, affirmations and visualisation are central practices.

A peak experience is a signal from Siggy to Napoleon of what you can do with focused attitudes and high expectations. If you've had a peak experience—and it's no coincidence that the term sounds orgasmic—relive the event in your imagination and make it part of your movie-making process as you settle down to visualise your way to a future dazzling performance. A peak experience makes it easier to believe your higher expectation of success because you know that if you've done it once, you can do it again.

Grant Fox's first peak experience came in 1984, when he was playing for the North Island team, coached by legendary lock Colin 'Pinetree' Meads, against the South Island at Rotorua. Meads' confidence in Fox, at a time when other top selectors were still wondering if the youngster really had the goods, and tactical help from John Hart (coach of Auckland at the time), combined to trigger that on-field sense of invulnerability that is one of the hallmarks of the peak experience. Fox kicked five conversions and three penalties that day to guide the North to a 39–3 thrashing of the South. Of that experience, Fox later wrote in his memoirs: 'I felt so in control of my game that day at Rotorua, deeply involved but somehow detached. It was the sort of game all of us want to have all the time but which, for all the complicated reasons which make rugby and individuals what they are, we too rarely experience.' This is a fine description of the peak experience, with the critical words being 'deeply involved but somehow detached'.

Expectation of success—having it, and/or developing it so that it induces peak experiences on demand—is what this book is about. It follows that one of the first myths to be denied is that this expectation (the level of confidence) is a factor of performance, that your confidence can increase only if you perform well. It just doesn't work that way.

The reverse is true: performance is a factor of expectation, and you don't start performing well until you confidently expect to. You always perform to your expectations, but you succeed only when you expect to succeed. *To raise the performance, crank up the expectations.*

The expectation index

At the start of the season you have imprinted on your subconscious a good idea of where you rank among players. As an exercise in the dynamics of expectation, try converting this ranking to an index number, one that reflects your standing within your team, and/or within the competition you play. If the highest score is +10 for a world-class player like Fox, and the lowest is −10 for an all-time flop, the rest of us fall somewhere in between, clustered around the average player at 0 on the scale. Give yourself the appropriate ranking.

For the purposes of this demonstration, let's extend the top of the range to +15, because the fact of the matter is that even a player of Fox's calibre can improve his level of expectation.

As the season progresses, we'd expect a player ranked +1 to improve through experience and practice to perhaps +2 at the end of the season. The level of performance will have varied during the season but the average would describe a growth line from +1 to +2, as on graph (a) below.

This is the growth pattern typical of a player who assesses his ranking on the basis of his performance. He still believes it's 'how you play on the day' that determines success, and he'll wait and

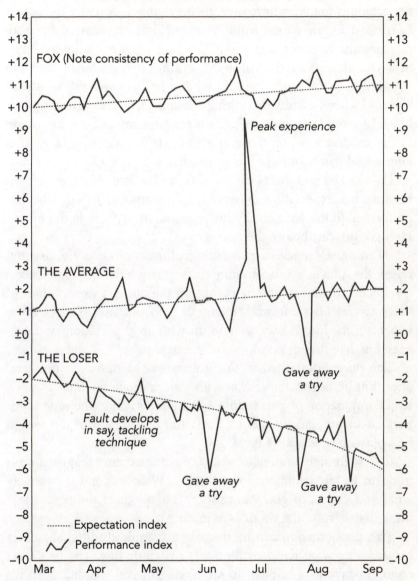

Expectation and Performance Graph (a)

see what happens on the day, before he decides what level of success to expect. Because he believes his ranking is a factor of his performance, he's vulnerable to both form slumps and good patches. He develops naturally enough through practice and experience, has his ups and downs and may even have a peak experience at some stage, as in graph (a), but because he moulds his expectations to his performance, he inevitably follows his index line of modest improvement from +1 to +2 over the season. He may produce the occasional shocker of a game, but his attitude of 'it's how you play on the day' probably ensures he's resilient enough to come back to the index line. If he has a hot run he'll follow it with a period when he fluffs everything—and back he comes to his index line. His attitude ensures he limits his improvement over the season to the modest level on the graph line. He'll make up lost ground after a bad patch and lose his gains after a good spell.

He's locked into this cycle and this modest level of improvement because his expectation of success is determined by how he has performed in the past, not by his potential to perform in the future. He's got the cart before the horse.

By contrast, the use of goal-setting, affirmations and visualisation raises the player's subconscious index number—his expectation level. This mental technique cranks up the player's expectations of success, and his performance cannot help but rise to meet those expectations. In this way we end up with an expectation/performance line like that in graph (b) on the next page.

The player described in this graph is a +1 based on performance, but he begins the season with his expectations inflated to +3 by a combination of goal-setting, affirmations and visualisation. His performance begins at the +1 level, but by the end of the season he's playing at +3 or +4 level.

It's a seemingly unbreakable law of human nature that we always perform to our confident expectations. What you get is precisely what you expect to get. Want more? Then expect more, and you immediately raise the chances of getting it.

This phenomenon can be described graphically to goal-kickers by watching what happens on a wet or windy day. The two most common sayings you hear about kicking in bad weather are: 'It's the same for everyone', and 'The weather's a great leveller'.

The first statement is undeniably true: wind and rain do affect the goal-kickers on both teams, but since they play one half with the wind and the other half against it, and the rain falls equally on all parts of the pitch, neither kicker has an advantage. But the first saying is contradicted by the second. 'The weather is a great leveller' begs

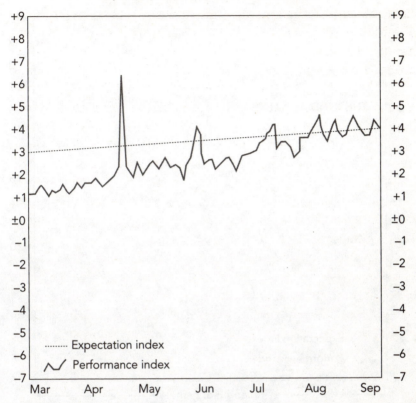

Expectation and Performance Graph (b)

the question of how, if the conditions are exactly the same for both kickers, the weather can make a raffle of their respective successful kicking rates. We begin to understand how this misconception has developed when we chart it, as in graph (c) on the next page.

Here we have two kickers, one with an expectation index based on his performance history of, say, +5, and the other with a performance/expectation index of +1. Assuming conditions are good, if both players have a similar desire to win, both are playing at their usual levels, and both players get an equal number of kicking opportunities, the +5 player will convert more of them to points than the +1 player.

But what happens to the expectation of success of the +5 player whose confidence suffers in the face of bad playing conditions? His expectation of success declines as a result, to perhaps +2.

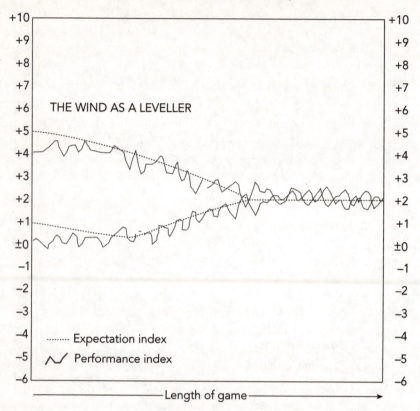

Expectation and Performance Graph (c)

THE WIND AS A LEVELLER

········ Expectation index
∧∨ Performance index

Length of game

The +1 player, detecting the decline in confidence/performance of the +5 player, automatically increases his own level of expectation of success from, say, +1 to +2. And suddenly their expectation indexes are equal.

Consequently, since performance mirrors expectation, they'll find themselves kicking equally well—or badly—and if the outcome of the game is dependent on the kicks, then it has indeed been reduced to a lottery. The weather has been a great leveller, but only because both of them expected it to be.

If a kicker believes that the weather is a great leveller, then the better that kicker normally performs, the further his confidence has to drop when the weather is bad. Conversely, the inferior kicker's expectations rise as soon as he realises the other kicker can't handle the conditions. If the second kicker's expectations rise above the falling expectations of his usually superior opponent, you've got a potential upset on your hands.

So the weather, in itself, is not a great leveller. What it does do though, is to offer a golden opportunity for the lower-ranked player—if he knows the relationship between performance and expectation—to give his team a kicking edge over the opposition with the higher-ranked player who remains naive enough to believe the weather is a great leveller. Anyone who believes the weather is a great leveller will perform in accordance with that belief and expectation—and will get levelled.

The hometown syndrome

A further illustration of how performance follows expectation is the home-and-away, or hometown, syndrome.

It's almost an article of faith in both codes of rugby that there's a huge advantage in playing at home—and statistics bear this out. But really, what's the difference? It's not the ability of the teams, which, all things being equal, stays the same no matter where they play. The supposed advantage of playing at home lies in the support of the spectators and familiarity with the environment. But how can fans and the environment affect the performance of the players? Fans don't take part in the game and the environment is the same for both teams. The outcome is decided on the playing field, not in the grandstand.

The hometown syndrome is so pervasive throughout rugby—indeed, throughout most sports—that it's worth taking a closer look at it, because it offers special opportunities for the goal-setting, affirming visualiser.

Rugby league, with its long history of professionalism, is statistically famous/notorious for conferring a huge hometown advantage, so let's take a look at a coach in that code who was famous (or notorious) for exploiting it. The coach is a New Zealander, the country is Australia, the competition is the State of Origin series, and we choose it as an example because league's longstanding professionalism should have (but hasn't) evened out the hometown advantage over time.

Australia's National Rugby League competition is probably where the code reaches its highest and most intense form (though players and fans of the British league are welcome to argue with that). Every week of the normal competition season, players from all round Australia and New Zealand, plus a few from the United Kingdom, Papua-New Guinea and the Pacific Islands, dutifully turn out for the clubs that pay them their handsome wages, and they perform to a uniformly high level. The players' loyalty to the clubs is overwhelmingly a factor of the money the clubs pay them. If a new club pays them more, they'll play just as well as, or better than, they did at the old club.

But then along comes the State of Origin series. It's a best-of-three format, confined solely to Australian players, and essentially between just two state teams, one from New South Wales, the other from Queensland. At State of Origin time the game suddenly takes on a personal complexion because, as well as the honour (and the extra money) of being chosen for an elite team, the players are representing their families and friends—their homes. Broadly speaking, the New South Wales players are city boys from Sydney, the heart of the code in Australia, while the Queensland players are country boys from the north. The resultant intensity of the State of Origin games is legendary.

In the early 1990s, Queensland hired for the series a coach who wasn't even an Australian, let alone a Queenslander. He was Graeme Lowe, a New Zealander noted for the big emphasis he put on the mental preparation of his players, and for playing mind games (often through the news media) with the opposition. For Lowe, the state of the player's mind was at least as important as his physical fitness and skill. Lowe was not the only rugby league coach who thought this way, nor the only one with a reputation for producing upsets, but we've chosen him for our example of how to manipulate the home-and-away syndrome because he was from neither New South Wales nor Queensland: he was just a pro hired for the series by a desperate Queensland management.

Queensland had good reason to feel desperate: its team comprised an injury-prone bunch of inexperienced kids, rounded out by a couple of ancient backline warriors overdue for retirement. New South Wales, by contrast, was virtually the Australian team, in peak condition and massively favoured by the media and the bookies to win.

But Graeme Lowe knew about the home-and-away syndrome, and he exploited it to the full. The first game was played on Queensland's home ground of Lang Park in Brisbane and Lowe's strategy was to expand in his young players' minds the notion—entirely fictional, as we've pointed out—that playing at home gives an advantage. He told his bunch of kids and geriatrics that somehow they would be transformed into supermen simply by putting on the maroon Queensland jersey and walking out onto Lang Park. To the local media Lowe chanted an endless refrain of hometown advantage, and it rapidly became a theme that Queenslanders at large picked up on, through personal contact and the media itself, and fed back to the players.

By the time the Queensland side took the field, Lowe had duped them into believing that they were certain to win, their overwhelming underdog status notwithstanding, because the hometown syndrome conferred invincibility on them. And, living up to their own (baseless) expectations, Queensland pulled off a huge upset and won first up.

The second game was in Sydney, on New South Wales turf, and for this away game Lowe turned his original psychological thrust completely upside down: blandly ignoring everything he'd told his players about the hometown advantage, he now began to feed them the line that, since they'd won on their home ground, there was no reason why they couldn't win away. This was probably too big and obvious a lie for the two old backline warriors, Wally Lewis and Mal Meninga, to swallow—they'd been around far too long—but the youngsters in the side fell for it hook, line and sinker. The result was that the team came within a whisker of beating New South Wales at home.

Lowe's strategy for the third and deciding match, back in Queensland, was to revert to his original lie—namely that there was a huge advantage in playing at home. This time he was able to reinforce the nonsense by pointing out two things. Firstly, Queensland had won the first home game against the bookies' odds, so logically they could do it again. Secondly, he told his team that the pundits and the form cards had been entirely wrong about them all along: New South Wales wasn't the better team after all—how could they be, since New South Wales had lost the first game, and had only just scraped home in the second despite having the insuperable advantage of playing at home?

Now to you and to me the scope of Graeme Lowe's gall would seem to know no bounds, but this is to overlook Lowe's appraisal of the task that faced him. His team was mostly young and inexperienced, so they were therefore highly suggestible—only the old battlers Lewis and Meninga would have seen through Lowe's strategy, and they were too smart to say anything.

What Lowe knew was that hometown advantage is a myth that exists only in the minds of people inexperienced—or stupid—enough to believe it. The rules don't vary between home and away. The players don't vary between home and away. And they're all playing on the same field in the same weather. So what's the difference? Only what's in the mind and, as Lowe demonstrated then as well as on other occasions, what's in the mind can be manipulated to produce a desired result. Oh, and yes, Queensland did win the decider back home at Lang Park, and the bookies took a bath.

Whichever the rugby code, the trick is to know that you can give yourself a hometown advantage even when you're playing away. All you have to do is raise your expectation of success, and your performance will improve in response.

It's as if the expectation line on our graph has magnets on it, drawing the performance line inexorably towards it. Affirmations and visualisation will automatically raise your expectation level—whether or not you believe they will. You don't have to wait for your standard of play to improve: you only have to raise your standard of thinking, and your play must follow the same pattern of improvement.

Instead of waiting to see 'how you play on the day', ensure you'll play well by feeding your subconscious with positive messages. Think about winning and how to win, and you'll be in the best possible shape to win.

The next time you have a peak experience, write about it when you get home. How did it feel? What happened to spark it? How good was it? Thereafter a peak experience will be the only performance on which you'll base your expectation index. All performances, other than the peak experience, are simply evidence of what you can do when you're not at your best.

Look at performance in this light and you'll find it's easy to get your expectation of success up where it belongs. You'll discover the secret by which every winner, every champion, performs to their highest potential.

When Grant Fox played that inter-island game in Rotorua, he discovered the notion of the peak experience because his expectation of success had been driven to its highest possible level by what Meads and Hart told him before the game. Also, he had chosen his options and kicked his goals so many times in his head that, as far as he was concerned, the game was won before the referee blew the whistle to start. With his expectation index so high, was it any surprise that his performance rose to the occasion? It was a surprise to him at the time. It was only later, when he had come to understand the dynamics of peak experiences, that he stopped being surprised at his ability to produce the big performance to meet the big occasion.

Using the same techniques will ensure that, on your big occasion, you too will not be surprised by the magic of the peak experience. And neither the weather nor the home-and-away syndrome will have anything to do with it.

– 12 –
The grand paradox meets the Grant Fox place kick

> You may not have what you long for till you cease to crave. **RACHEL McALPINE**

Throughout our lives we're programmed to believe that the harder we try the more successful we become. We're told, 'If at first you don't succeed, try, try again.' Yet here we are with a book that guarantees improvement in your game, but on the basis that you don't try. How, you might ask, in a game like rugby that makes massive demands on players' stamina—not to mention their skill, resilience, foresight and all the rest of it—can you play without trying? Surely there's a contradiction, a grand paradox, in there somewhere?

No, there ain't. The reality is that the harder you try consciously —that is, the harder Napoleon tries to impose his will on Siggy—the less successful you're likely to be. And that goes for all sport, not just rugby.

The principle of all training, physical and mental, is to remove the need to try consciously to perform well on the day. You remove the need by stocking up your Siggy's hard disk with files of all the data he's likely to need *before* he's called on to perform, and by stocking up your body with the stamina and muscular capacity necessary for physical performance.

But once you get out there on the field, the concept of trying gives way to the concept of applying.

To help unravel this grand paradox, let's take another look at distance runners—say, milers (as 1500-metre runners still like to be called). In a race, they run themselves to the limit of their stamina, suffering increasingly from oxygen debt as they approach the finish. Their aim is to use up every bit of energy they've got stored in their bodies, but not before they reach the finish.

In the old days, before the links between mental preparation and physical performance began to be understood, you'd often see milers struggling their way up the final straight with their arms clutching at the air and their faces screwed up like Mr Ugly contestants, because they still believed that there was a direct connection between pain and performance—that the more they hurt, the better they performed.

The reality is the opposite. Pain may be an inescapable by-product of running fast over a distance, but there's no direct relationship between the amount of pain you suffer and your success or otherwise in a running race. It's quite possible to run a fast mile with hardly any pain at all, and a modern master like Hicham El Guerrouj is a picture of effortless motion as he prances up the straight to another world record. Effect without conscious effort—that's the formula.

The prescription for success in running, as in rugby, is to try to succeed by not consciously trying. The Zen masters of Japan call this paradox 'effortless effort'.

Let's break the prescription down into two parts: (a) 'try to succeed' by (b), 'not consciously trying'. The first part, (a), means you should be determined to succeed by building your desire along with your physical capacity to win, while (b) means you should learn not to let Napoleon interfere with the work Siggy does when it comes to applying the mental and physical capacities developed through training.

Setting goals, writing affirmations and practising awareness are—like skill and stamina training—all (a) procedures. They'll build up your desire and determination. This is the 'effort' part of 'effortless effort'. After all, if you didn't want to try to play to your potential (that is, to make an effort), why bother playing? Your time might be better spent in the garden where, of course, you'd simply be trying something else.

The problem with (a)-type trying is that we tend to assume that tight mental control is necessary to express a physical skill. To put it another way, (a)-type trying is often misconstrued as a need for Napoleon to exercise conscious effort constantly in order to get the best out of Siggy. That, in turn, implies that Napoleon is in some way superior to Siggy in his capacity to influence the muscle and nerve movements. It implies also that Napoleon needs to instruct Siggy in what to do—that Napoleon is the 'general' ordering Siggy, the 'soldier', into battle.

Forget it: that just ain't the way it works at all. Napoleon and Siggy are not master and servant, but equal partners. Each has his own separate and distinct abilities and limitations which, if allowed to, mesh perfectly to produce perfect results.

The thing about Siggy is that he's the perfect soldier: he'll obey instructions to the letter, even if those instructions stop him from doing the job Napoleon really wants him to do. El Guerrouj coming up the straight is pure Siggy. He cut his Napoleon out of the performance loop about half a lap back when the need to think tactically, to practise awareness, gave way to unleashing Siggy to perform the final dash to the tape. By the time El Guerrouj hits the straight, the race is already won or lost. There's no longer any need for Napoleon to feed information to Siggy, because Siggy's operating under his final instructions: 'get to the tape as fast as possible'. At this point there is nothing Napoleon can do to enhance Siggy's performance, so Napoleon is deliberately cut out of the performance loop. Indeed, if Napoleon were to remain active at this stage, bombarding Siggy with instructions to 'try harder', he'd deflect Siggy from his real purpose of maximising speed, and instead persuade him to maximise pain. The winner is the one who crosses the line first, not the one who suffers most in getting there.

When Grant Fox began to take rugby seriously, he quickly became aware of the essential paradox of sports psychology: try too hard and you end up performing below your optimum. Or, to put it another way, the harder you try the worse you perform.

This realisation was particularly important to Foxy because of the intense, perfectionist sort of person he is. He was the perfect candidate to tense up, not so much with the pressure of the game as with the desire to play well and win. Fox regarded himself as having little natural talent—he scoffed at his own light build and made jokes about his bandy legs—and his prescription for getting to the top of his game was plain old hard work, for which another word is 'effort'. To provide another string to his bow, to make himself more attractive to selectors at all levels, Fox took up place-kicking. He figured selectors might overlook the noisy bloke bellowing instructions to the backline from first-five, but they couldn't overlook him if he was averaging a dozen or more points a game with his goal-kicking. And, in taking up goal-kicking, Fox learned the grand paradox of 'effortless effort'.

Unlike everything else in rugby, place-kicking requires no stamina—indeed the physical element in kicking is minimal. It was through kicking that Fox discovered the separate and distinct roles of Siggy the supercomputer, and Napoleon the computer operator —and the need to keep them separate and distinct.

In 1971 New Zealanders hooted and jeered when some Pommie first-five, as he was initially referred to, pirouetted through a tight S-bend in his place-kicking run-up. They didn't laugh for long, though. The 'Pommie first-five' was actually Welsh, the inimitable fly half Barry John, and by the time he'd finished silencing New Zealand crowds that year, John had amassed 180 points for a brilliant Lions touring team that thrashed the All Blacks in a four-test home series.

One Kiwi who neither jeered nor laughed, but watched John intently every time he got to see him kick, was a skinny little blond-haired kid off a sheep farm near Waotu in the Waikato. The skinny kid was Grant James Fox, aged nine.

Fox went on to become one of the first goal-kickers in top New Zealand rugby to use Barry John's round-the-corner, hit-it-with-your-instep technique. From early on it was apparent to Fox that the kicking leg in round-the-corner place kicks operates in the same way as the club in golf—similar trajectory, similar plane. It followed that place-kickers should address the rugby ball the same way golfers do the golf ball.

But it was not until 1984, the year he made the All Blacks for the first time, that Fox got effective advice from Jim Blair, the New Zealand rugby fitness specialist, on how he should address the ball for a place kick. It was Blair who taught Fox the relationship between relaxation and breathing, covered earlier in this book, and together they developed Fox's signature kicking ritual.

We'll analyse both Fox's breathing and kicking techniques shortly, but first let's examine the principles behind Jim Blair's breathing ritual in the light of our understanding of the very distinct and separate roles of Siggy and Napoleon. Even though Fox had never heard of Siggy and Napoleon in those days, his application of Blair's breathing technique had the effect of turning responsibility for his kicks over to his internal computer, his Siggy. As his Siggy took over, Fox's goal-kicking took on the effortlessness which was the hallmark of his game. In the act of organising his breathing to induce relaxation, Fox entrusted his Siggy with the kicking job. And pressure, doubt and fear of failure—all the things that make a kicker miss—melted away.

Precision kicking and all the other skills of rugby involve co-ordination of muscle movements of a complexity you couldn't possibly approach by conscious thought. Yet throwing thought out the window is a mighty difficult exercise for an adult human being. The ego (another term for Napoleon) has such a high opinion of itself that it has trouble accepting that Siggy can handle a pressure situation perfectly well without Napoleon's help.

When things aren't going well during a game, Napoleon tends to demand more and more precautionary control. 'I must concentrate,' he says. 'I must try harder.' The more Napoleon thinks like this, the more control he wants to exert over Siggy. But—and here again is our grand paradox—the more control he assumes over Siggy, the worse Siggy performs.

The challenge for rugby goal-kickers is compounded by the fact that, prior to lining up the ball, they've been dashing round the pitch under varying degrees of oxygen debt. They're puffing and panting and their pulses are racing from the frenetic physical activity, and now they suddenly have to become physically and mentally calm so they can execute the goal kick. It's not an easy transition to make, but the ability to do it is central to the success rate.

The Grant Fox place-kicking ritual

These days it's rare to see place-kickers use the old head-on approach to either the torpedo or the upright ball placement—where contact with the ball is made by the toe rather than the instep—but the Grant Fox round-the-corner leave-it-to-Siggy prekick ritual we describe here can be adapted to either of those techniques. The principle is the same, even though the techniques are different. (Fox himself started out as a boy with a torpedo toe kick from a head-on approach but, when he discovered the ball could be kicked equally accurately with the instep, he was more than delighted to make the switch. The reason? New Zealand children played much of their rugby in bare feet, which led to the kicker having chronic sore toes.)

Fox sums up his trademark round-the-corner place-kicking as 'a side-on craft, just like golf'. The aim is to swing your kicking leg precisely as you would a golf club. Another parallel with golf is the way you bring the line of your shoulders round to aim at the target at the moment of contact with the ball. In kicking, unlike golf, the arms are employed primarily for balance, though the one nearer the goal also serves as an aiming device: at the moment of contact with the ball, your goal-side arm should be an extension of the line of your shoulders, pointing directly at the target.

Fox's other fundamental kicking principle is to have a set routine that is exactly the same from one kick to the next. In terms of our in-built computer, Siggy, a set routine means he only has to store one single kicking information file on his hard disk—and practice and performance alike should serve simply to refine the information in that single file.

This unchanging routine should extend even to tiny details like the direction in which the valve of the ball faces. Before the advent of needle-nozzle pumps, rugby balls used to have a bulky lace that fully enclosed the bung, and it was an unwritten rule for place-kickers that the ball should be placed with the lace facing the goal. It makes no difference these days what direction you face the valve in, but it should be the same every time.

Another Fox principle is that the routine is strictly an individual one, and should not be a conscious copy of any other kicker's.

'Every individual should develop their own routine,' he says. 'Experiment to find what's comfortable for you, and work that experience into a routine that's exclusively your own.'

Fox extends the individual approach to the choice of tee. These days most tees are commercially made, but Fox has declined to endorse any one model because his own preference is for sand. He sees sand as having greater flexibility in dealing with such variables as wind, the length of the grass and the state of the ground underfoot. Fox has no objection to tees, commercial or home-made, insisting instead that the choice of kicking platform is a matter of individual preference. He accepts that what tees lack in terms of variable ball-placement they make up for in terms of consistency in the routine—and that's an all-important factor.

Ball placement

Fox prefers to place the ball as near to perfectly upright as possible. He acknowledges that many kickers, especially in rugby league, tilt the ball towards the goal, and that works for them. The key factor in choosing whether to have the ball upright or leaning towards the target is the need for the kicker to see the contact point throughout the run-up. To achieve this, taller players, like record-breaking Kiwi rugby league kicker Daryl Halligan, often need to lean the ball forwards. That factor aside, the only rule is that the ball must neither lean backwards, nor laterally to either the left or the right.

Taking aim

The modern four-panel ball invites aiming along the line of the seam, which creates a 'v' across the tip of the ball resembling the rear sight of a rifle. Fox's technique is to crouch on one knee behind the ball and line the seam and 'v-sight' up with the target, making adjustments to the ball with outstretched arms. In doing so he has the ball at the centre of his line of sight, and the goalposts within his peripheral vision. The disadvantage of the alternative—standing directly over the ball to line it up—is that it prevents the kicker from seeing both the ball and the goalposts at the same time. The way Fox does it, you can see both ball and target without moving your head up and down.

It's at this point that you factor in the wind: when there's no wind you aim your non-kicking foot at the centre of the crossbar. Kicking in windy conditions is covered on page 134.

Point of contact

The central point of contact, which must be visible throughout the run-up, should be 'just above the bottom point, about a quarter of the way up,' Fox says. It's this point—not the ball as a whole—that the kicker needs to focus on throughout the run-up, and it doesn't vary between long kicks and short ones.

Addressing the ball

Once the ball has been placed, the kicker needs to step back to check the aim, then return and address the ball. This firstly involves rehearsing the placement of the non-kicking foot (the left for right-footers, the right for left-footers). This is the key to consistent kicking, Fox says. Where you place the non-kicking foot dictates the positioning of the rest of your body in relation to the ball. For a right-foot kicker, the ball will follow the line of the instep of your left foot. So in addressing the ball, place your non-kicking foot so that your ankle lines up with the side seam of the ball, about half the width of your hips away from it, and with your foot pointing straight at the target. The line of your non-kicking foot is the line the ball will take in flight.

You complete the addressing of the ball by fixing your eyes on the central point of contact. Since you're standing over the ball at this stage, the central point of contact may be out of sight, depending on whether you prefer to lean the ball forward on the tee or to have it upright. Either way, the central point of contact will come fully into view again as you step back.

Pre-run-up positioning

Now step the several paces back to your pre-run-up position, without taking your eyes off the central point of contact on the ball. Fox's routine was to pace directly back from the ball, pause, then take two wide steps to the side, but he says it's a matter of choice whether the kicker reaches his pre-run-up position this way, or by stepping back on an angle from the ball.

It's also a matter of personal choice as to how many steps back you take. What is important is that you keep your eyes on the point of contact, and, above all, follow exactly the same routine for each kick.

The angle of the pre-run-up position from the intended trajectory of the ball is again a matter of personal choice. Some kickers take a shallow angle of perhaps 30 degrees, while others like one as sharp as 90 degrees. Within that range it's a case of whatever feels comfortable. 'There's no right or wrong angle to take,' Fox says. Fox's personal preference was for a shallower angle, one in which his sternum (breastbone) was pointing at the just-visible back seam of the ball. The only no-no would be to stand square-on to your target (that is, directly behind the ball). The simple principle is to aim your body at the back of the ball, and have the line of your shoulders aiming at the target.

Achieving balance

Once you've arrived at your pre-run-up position, stand with your feet slightly apart and directly under the line of your shoulders, just as a golfer would. The aim is to settle into almost perfect balance, something you can't do with your feet together, too far apart, or in a different vertical plane from your shoulders. If your feet are too close together, your weight will come forward onto your toes, and if they're too far apart your weight will shift back onto your heels. Your weight should be just fractionally forward of the balls of your feet.

Informing Siggy

Once in position on his starting point, the kicker lifts his eyes for the first time from the point of contact and looks at the target. Then back to the point of contact, up to the target, and finally back to the point of contact again. This looking at the target is a crucial factor: it's pure awareness, feeding uncluttered information to Siggy on the relative positions of both the ball and the goalposts. Napoleon should be feeding Siggy every scrap of empirical (measurable) information he can absorb: the distance to the posts, the angle of trajectory—even the temperature. It's all absorbed and transmitted by that process of being aware, which is observation without interpretation. You don't need Napoleon saying, 'Golly, it's a long way to the posts' or 'Gee, it's so hot I'm uncomfortable' or, worst of all, 'This is a vital kick so you better not miss it.' That's all grubby, cluttering information, and Siggy's got no good use for it.

Visualising

In this process the kicker needs to employ that vital tool, visualisation. While looking from the ball to the posts, the kicker needs to 'see' the ball lift from the tee and sail between the posts. Of course the ball is not really moving at all—it's waiting for you right there on the tee—but it's a key skill of the kicker to have his mind's eye rehearse the ball's trajectory before it has even been kicked. And this rehearsal, essentially an information-gathering exercise, has to take place with the eyes open. It's a case of getting the mind's eye to superimpose the ball's intended trajectory upon what the eyes are seeing. It sounds like a contradiction, an impossibility, but it's a skill Napoleon is perfectly capable of developing. This 'seeing' of something which is not actually occurring is simply awareness taken to a higher, purer level. It's the ultimate form of communication from Napoleon to Siggy.

The breathing exercise

Either during this visualisation process, or after your eyes have returned to the point of contact for the final time, the breathing exercise can be introduced to the routine. Take a long, unhurried breath in, filling the lungs to capacity, then breathe out just as slowly till your lungs are empty. As you expel all that air, be conscious—aware—that you're also expelling all stress and tension. Feel the stress and tension drain out of you. Fox reinforced this awareness by giving that characteristic waggling of his fingers, as if he was shaking the last bits of tension out of his body—which was, in fact, precisely what he was doing.

Repeat the breathing exercise if you like, the important thing being to keep your routine identical from kick to kick.

As we learned earlier in this book, one of the aims of this breathing exercise is to slow the pattern of brain waves from the usual adult beta pattern of between 14 and 40 cycles a second, to the baby's pattern of between 8 and 13 a second. It's at the slower pattern that Siggy performs best.

Switching Napoleon off

The breathing exercise also serves as the signal to Napoleon that his job is finished for the time being, and he's being switched off. Napoleon has completed his job of giving Siggy all that pure and uncluttered information, and now he needs to close down and leave the execution of the kick up to Siggy.

The run-up

A round-the-corner kicker must get his body into a side-on position to kick the ball, so unless you're positioned very acutely to the ball—that is, close to 90 degrees—you're going to have to move to the left (to the right for a left-footer) if you're to arrive side-on to kick it. This is why your starting point, your angle from the intended trajectory of the ball, is not that important. What matters is that you arrive at the ball side-on to it—and hence the emphasis Fox places on the positioning of the non-kicking foot. Beginning with your non-kicking foot, you have to get that side of your body, and the line across your shoulders, all pointing at the target at the moment of contact with the ball. To get there from your starting position you have to approach the ball in a double arc—what Fox describes as 'an unfinished S-bend'—in your run-up.

The act of kicking a ball involves a transfer of your bodyweight through it. Your foot doesn't stop at the football, any more than a golf club stops when it hits the golf ball: the point of contact is just one point in the arc of the swing.

To transfer your bodyweight through the ball by way of a kick, your weight has to be on the balls of your feet, and the way to get it there is by having your head slightly ahead of your feet throughout the run-up, which requires you to start your run-up with small steps. Once you're under way, you lengthen your stride to build up the forward momentum that will project your weight through your kicking leg and through the ball. Keeping your head ahead of your feet keeps your weight on the balls of your feet. 'Never let yourself lean back on your heels, because once you're there you never recover,' Fox says.

Point of contact

The area of impact of your foot on the ball is quite large: it runs from your big toe along that high bone of your instep and up to the base of your shin. In fact, it's the biggest possible area of impact you can make between a 300mm-long oval ball and a human foot (which lends weight to the true rugby aficionado's contention that God designed the human foot specifically for kicking an oval football). And the bigger the area of impact, the more accurate the kick. It stands to reason: the bigger the area of impact, the more control you have over the behaviour of the ball.

At the moment of contact, your kicking-side shoulder has to be rotating forward to where both shoulders line up with the target. You achieve this by having your non-kicking-side hand and arm (the left side for right-footers) point at the target. This has the effect of pulling the opposite shoulder forward into alignment, while at the same time maintaining the momentum through the point of contact between the ball and your foot. It also has the equally important effect of bringing your hips side-on to the ball—which is where they need to be to allow your kicking leg to make its full rotation through the point of contact, thereby generating maximum power and control. Again there are close parallels with golf in this shoulder-driven rotation of the hips. To deliver maximum power, your hips need to go through a 90-degree rotation, which in turn requires you to be side-on to the intended trajectory of the ball. If instead you get more or less square-on to the target, you'll be able to rotate your hips through only, say, 45 degrees—which has the effect of halving the potential power of the stroke.

Controlling the draw

Allowing that full 90-degree rotation of the hips and shoulders not only lends power to the stroke, but also allows you to control the draw (the ball's tendency to curl inwards in flight—from right to left in the case of a right-footer), which is a by-product of the round-the-corner technique. Most kickers are happy to allow this draw, this curl, to occur naturally, and they simply adjust their aim to take it into account. Drawing the ball this way tends to make it easier to kick goals from one side of the field than the other (the 'right' side and 'wrong' side that commentators refer to) depending on which foot you kick with. But by getting completely side-on to the line of trajectory, you can eliminate all draw and make the ball go in a dead-straight line.

The 'right' side of the field for a right-footer is the left side of the field. When the right-footed kick is taken from a position to the left of the goalposts, the kicker is able to employ the draw to improve his chances of success. That's because, as the ball curls round right-to-left through the arc of the draw, it's necessarily widening the angle at which it approaches the goalposts. The goalposts are 5.6 metres apart, but when you're kicking from the sideline on the 22-metre mark, the target the posts offer is less than half (about 2.5 metres) what it is from head-on, so drawing the ball in an outward curve widens the target. That's the upside of the draw kick.

The downside comes into play for a right-footer kicking from a position on the right-hand side of the goalposts. From the right-hand sideline 22 metres out, the target starts out being more than halved in width, but is further narrowed if the ball's trajectory takes it closer to the goal line. Depending on how pronounced the draw is, your actual target could be as narrow as 1 metre. And since your actual distance from the centre of the crossbar is all of 40 metres, that's a mighty small target. So any advantage you gain by drawing the ball in an arc from your 'right' side becomes just as big a disadvantage when you have to attempt a kick from your 'wrong' side. Figure 1 shows the trajectories from 'right' and 'wrong' sides of the field. Figure 2 shows the angles offered from each side of the field.

Accordingly, you improve your chances of overall success by eliminating the draw and kicking the ball dead straight.

While Grant Fox would be the first to admire a beautifully drawn kick that curves round to bisect the crossbar, he stresses the advantage of having a single routine for every kick, rather than having to develop two routines—one for the draw from your 'right' side, and one for the straight kick from your 'wrong' side. For the sake of consistency, Fox says, it's better to kick every kick straight. After all, you get no more points for a beautifully curved kick than for a plain old straight one.

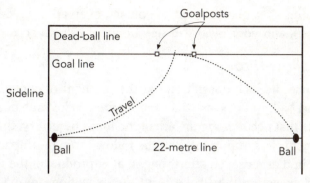

Figure 1: The effects of the draw or curl of the round-the-corner placekick. Taken by a right-footed kicker from the left side of the field, the draw opens up the angle at which the ball approaches the posts, increasing its chance of success. But when the kick is taken from the right-hand side of the field, the angle of approach narrows, so reducing the chance of success.

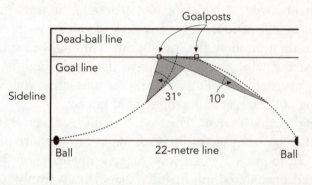

Figure 2: The shaded areas demonstrate how wide the angle of trajectory becomes for a right-footed kicker kicking from the left-hand side of the field, and how narrow it becomes when the kick has to be taken from the right-hand side of the field. Moral of the story? Learn to minimise the draw, Fox says, thereby straightening the ball's trajectory and giving yourself equal chance of success whichever side of the field the kick is taken from.

Carriage of the head

A 'rule' that kickers hear endlessly is, 'Keep your head down'. It's true that if your head comes up before the moment of impact, you'll fluff the kick, usually by 'topping' it. But what dictates the position of your head is the focus of your eyes, and from the moment you start your run-up your eyes must be fastened on the point of contact.

Keep your eyes on the point of contact, even after the ball has left your foot, and your head will stay down of its own accord.

The follow-through

Of course the kick doesn't end at the moment of contact between foot and ball. In the sense that that moment is just one of an infinite number that occur along the arc of the foot's trajectory, the moment of impact is less important than the follow-through. Impact with the ball is, in that sense, an afterthought, a by-product of the main business of executing the stroke. And the execution doesn't end until the foot has completed its full arc, at about eye-level.

In summary, the single most important aspect of a successful place kick is getting the leading side of your body in the right position, and the single most important factor in achieving that is the final placement of your non-kicking foot. 'Forget about what you do with the trailing side of your body,' Fox says. 'If you get your leading side into the right position, the trailing side will follow naturally. Don't worry about what your trailing arm does—it'll find its own way about. Just get that leading arm, and the line across your shoulders, pointing at the target at the moment of impact.'

'Get these basics right,' Fox says, 'and there's no pressure on you, no matter how important the kick might be. Pressure just doesn't exist.' Or, to put it another way, Siggy is operating on the basis of pure and uncluttered information, Napoleon is firmly locked into the 'Off' mode, and you've just scored a further two or three points.

Kicking in the wind

The key to accurate kicking in the wind is, once again, awareness. You need to consciously tune your Napoleon to gather every bit of pure and uncluttered information he can about the two wind factors that will influence the ball's trajectory: strength and direction. Both can vary markedly during the short space of time it takes to set the ball up, check your aim, correct it, address the ball and kick it.

If the whole operation takes a minute, you get only 30 seconds—the time between placing the ball and finalising your aim—to gather information on how much allowance to make for the wind.

The critical information-gathering time for Napoleon is after you've stepped back from placing the ball, while you're eyeing it up for final adjustments to its aim and attitude. During these vital seconds, Napoleon should be going through a set data-gathering routine. Start at ground-level, noting the effect the wind is having on the blades of grass round the ball, then progressively raise and broaden your scope of awareness to take in the sideline marker-flags, before moving on up to any tree-tops, awnings, flags, smoke or cloud movement. Then, just as deliberately and progressively, work your way back to ground level again.

Be aware during this time that wind-speed will vary at different heights, as well as different times: generally, the higher the ball is kicked, the stronger the winds it will encounter.

Also be aware of the wind's potential to swirl like a whirlpool, and for the centre of the whirlpool to shift rapidly about the playing area. This effect is particularly marked in stadiums, whether they are fully or partially enclosed.

The wind in each stadium and around each pitch performs differently. You'll learn a lot about your home ground by practising there, and it's a good idea to keep written notes on every ground at which you play. Ask other kickers and informed locals about wind behaviour on particular pitches.

Having absorbed all that information, Siggy, your personal in-built computer, is ready for the two calculations he has to make. First he decides how wind speed and direction will affect the ball in flight, then how far left or right of the centre of the crossbar to aim the ball. With those decisions made, you return to the ball and adjust it accordingly.

After you've moved to your run-up starting point, the adjusted aiming point—which might be anywhere along the crossbar, or on the same plane but outside the posts—becomes the focus of the visualisation exercises you perform as you finally address the ball.

Having kicked, don't immediately switch Napoleon off or cease gathering information. Keep watching the ball closely throughout its flight and be aware of the effects the wind has on it. This is vital for your next kick. It's immaterial to Siggy whether or not the kick is successful: the important thing is that Siggy absorbs and files away the knowledge the ball makes available during its flight.

The step-kick exercise

Should you still find yourself having difficulty cutting Napoleon out of the loop, especially when there's a lot riding on the kick, a technique that will help is the step-kick exercise, which has parallels with the supercharger exercise that we introduced in Chapter 10. You'll remember that the supercharger was aimed especially—though not exclusively—at forwards in those all too few glorious moments when they suddenly find themselves with the ball in hand and a couple of metres to run before they disappear once again into the ruck or maul. The supercharger was triggered by a prearranged —'prerecorded', if you like—yell or grunt, with the player at the same time stamping his foot into the ground as he launches himself at the opposition. The aim is to trigger a sudden extra rush of adrenalin, by letting Siggy know that here we have a special occasion when he's got to explode towards the opposition with every ounce of energy and aggression in his reservoirs.

The supercharger is a variant on anchoring, and so is the step-kick exercise that we've devised especially for place-kickers. Try this out in practice first, and when you've proved to yourself that it works, use it in a game. The aim, as always, is to trust Siggy totally, and to cut Napoleon out of the performance loop regardless of the scoreboard or the difficulty of the kick.

1. Look at the goalposts and visualise the perfect kick sailing between them over the middle of the crossbar.
2. Consciously turn the job totally over to Siggy.
3. As your lead or non-kicking foot lands alongside the ball at the end of your run-up, say out loud (or under your breath), '*step*'. Then, at the exact moment of contact between your instep and the ball, say '*kick*'.

By saying 'step' and 'kick', you're transferring your conscious thoughts into an area where they won't interfere with the way Siggy kicks the shot you visualised. If you're consciously thinking of this timing exercise you won't be overly concerned with the result: there'll be no self-doubt, no fear of failure or anything else to strangle your potential to kick the goal.

To pass or to run: the respective decisions of Joost van der Westhuizen for South Africa (above) against Australia and Justin Marshall for the All Blacks against Tonga were effectively taken long before either halfback took the field, when they stacked their Siggys' hard-disks with options created by affirmation and visualisation.

The scoreboard tells the story of what was arguably Zinzan Brooke's finest game for the All Blacks against South Africa. Brooke opened a new chapter in No. 8 play through the range of skill-files he stacked into his personal, inbuilt computer.

Durable All Black prop Craig Dowd heads for RICE treatment. Tolerance of pain and recovery from injury are directly affected by mental attitude.

Support of the ball-carrier is a reflexive response that must be emblazoned on Siggy's hard-disk. In these All Black pictures, Jeff Wilson (centre) finds himself stranded against Australia, but Justin Marshall and Josh Kronfeld are in close support of Tana Umaga against Scotland (top), and there's plenty of help on hand for Jonah Lomu (bottom) as he leads the charge against Australia.

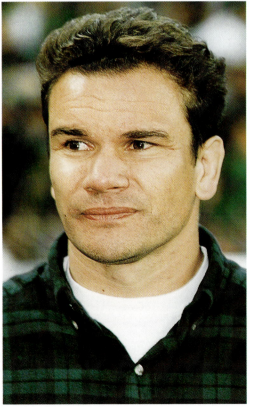

Gamesmanship is a great and useful skill, but you don't have to be a great gamer to be a great rugby player. The foremost gamer of modern rugby, All Black captain Sean Fitzpatrick (above, with long-time cohort Olo Brown) took particular delight in tormenting South African teams and spectators alike, but fellow Aucklander Michael Jones achieved comparable greatness, and almost saintlike popularity, precisely because he never indulged in gamesmanship.

This exercise will demonstrate that the road to success lies in banishing the ego (Napoleon) from the performance delivery system. Results are, in a sense, meaningless: goal-kicking and rugby are experiences—nothing more, nothing less. If you want results, stop worrying about them and you'll find they come in a rush.

Goal-kicking, possibly more than any other single rugby skill, teaches you how to tap your hidden potential by trusting Siggy (your non-conscious self). Overconcern with the result of the kick decreases the chances of success. Overconcern is simply Napoleon attempting to control Siggy—and that's a job that Napoleon simply isn't equipped for.

–13–
Harnessing fear, managing pain

> The greatest fear is of failure, and the greatest pain is of losing. **Grant Fox**

Rugby is a physical contact sport, so you can expect to get injured from time to time—and that's part of the attraction of the game. This doesn't mean you have to be a masochist to play rugby—no one in their right mind plays specifically to get hurt. But pain, both physical and emotional, is an unavoidable by-product of rugby, as of life.

That being the case, and given that no entirely sane person actually enjoys pain, why play a game in which injury and pain are endemic? The answer is that the risks involved in playing rugby reflect something in our mental make-up—probably some innate drive to demonstrate our fitness to survive—that demands we take otherwise avoidable or unnecessary emotional and/or physical risks.

Back in the bad old days this craving for risk found its highest expression in warfare. It is really only in the last couple of generations that warfare has lost its attraction to humans, in part because the nuclear age has made the risks unacceptably high, and in part because the information revolution has taken the romance out of slaughter and destruction. In reality, war was never valiant or glorious—it was rarely even honourable or dignified, and then only for the winners—but we maintained romantic notions about it as long as we could reasonably expect that our opponents would suffer more pain and death from it than we would. Television and the nuclear age of mutually assured destruction have thankfully knocked those quaint notions on the head.

But they haven't eliminated the human hunger for danger and risk, and these days the ultimate combative risks within civilised and developed societies are to be found in contact sports, where the rules ensure a more or less even spread of the risk across all participants. That risk-hunger can be satiated individually in martial arts, or collectively in team contact sports, of which the rugby codes are arguably the riskiest.

The risks of playing rugby can be easily quantified. In New Zealand, which has a population of about 3.75 million (the same as Ireland's) and regards rugby union as its national sport, 135,000 people (3.6 per cent of the population) of both sexes play the game. In any given year, about 5500 of them (barely 1 in 25) can expect to be injured seriously enough to need time off work, compensation or rehabilitation. Deaths directly related to rugby union occur at the rate of perhaps one a year, while between 1996 and 1999 four players (that is, another one per year) became paraplegics or quadriplegics, mostly as the result of scrum collapses. Your chance of being seriously injured or killed playing rugby in New Zealand is thus about 1 in 67,500 per year. Considering New Zealand roads can account for up to 500 deaths a year (that is, 1 for every 7500 people), you're about nine times safer playing a game of rugby than you are travelling to and from it.

Rugby players don't take the field specifically to get injured, but rather to flout the risk of it. The upside of flouting that risk without serious injury is the glorious sense of achievement and satisfaction that comes from successfully defying odds, the more so when you also happen to beat your opponent. This may not reflect the rosiest or most humane side of human nature, but many millennia will pass before we shake it off.

The downside of flouting the risk is that you may indeed get hurt physically—to which emotional hurt is added if your team also happens to get beaten. Not everything we do in life is risky, but the mere fact of living is life-threatening. So let's look more closely at these two unavoidable by-products of choosing to flout the risks involved in playing rugby: fear and pain.

Fear

At some point in their career, every rugby player encounters, and has to come to terms with, fear. There are essentially two kinds: fear of injury and fear of failure.

You generally encounter the fear of injury first, because of its immediacy, and of the two it's both the less useful and the easier to deal with. Injury fear also tends to be the more fleeting: once you've come to terms with it, it generally ceases to be a major problem.

Fear of failure, however, is a constantly recurring emotion and, as such, is your most powerful emotional ally. Yes, 'ally'.

Fear is a good thing. Fear is your friend. If you lack fear—and some people do—then you are seriously, perhaps life-threateningly, flawed. Or you simply haven't built up a strong enough desire to win, to succeed.

Fear derives from the strongest and most basic urge of all life forms: the desire to live. Thus, fear is the barometer of threat to life and if you don't experience it you ain't really living.

People who start rugby as preschoolers, as Grant Fox did, have generally sorted out their physical fear before they reach their teens. Sometimes this comes about by the simple process of getting used to, and blasé about, the bumps and bangs. Older starters often have to confront their physical fear, but once they have done so it generally ceases to be a problem.

If physical fear *is* a problem, the way to deal with it is first to own it. Don't despise or belittle yourself for being frightened of the physical contact; instead be grateful that you're smart and sensitive enough to realise that there is a risk and to minimise its downside.

Be aware that fear is a great servant, but a destructive master. Accordingly, you need to be in control of your fear, not at its mercy. Remember too that you have to feel fear to know courage, and that the courageous person is not the one who knows no fear, but the one who recognises and harnesses their fear and makes it work for them.

In dealing practically with physical fear, so that it's an aid rather than a drawback to your game, you need above all to be aware that the risk of being hurt actually rises in direct proportion to your lack of commitment to the physical contact. Put another way, the more wary you are of getting hurt in a full-contact sport, the more likely you are to get hurt. This is because Siggy gets confused, and his circuits get overloaded and mixed up, if Napoleon instructs him to apply anything less than total commitment to the physical contact. Siggy cannot be both committed and tentative at the same time. If Siggy gets confused signals—such as, 'Okay, tackle this guy but do it gently because he's big and might hurt us'—he'll deliver a confused performance. And when one party to a full-contact sport confuses his fight instincts with his flight instincts, he does both badly. It stands to reason: vastly more injuries occur as the result of poor performance—that is, poor execution of the basic skills—than of good performance. You're more likely to be hurt in a badly executed tackle than in a textbook one.

Siggy can't be both aggressive and passive at the same time: he can be only one or the other. He can either fight or flee, but he can't do both. So the way to harness and harvest your physical fear is to direct it towards requiring total physical commitment from Siggy, for the very reason that anything less than total commitment increases the risk of pain and injury.

Incorporate these rationales into your regular daily mental training by way of visualisation—see yourself flattening the ball-carrier with your big-hit tackle—and also into your pre-match ritual. You'll very quickly discover that your physical fears evaporate, to be replaced by fear only of failure.

Neither Fox nor any other high-level competitor ever loses their fear of failure. Nor would they ever want to. Those queasy pre-game feelings in the pit of the stomach—the 'butterflies' or the 'screaming willies'—are pure fear of failure, and Fox used to be just about tied up in knots by them before a big match. But he wouldn't be without them. They are the measure of the desire to win.

The trick to harnessing them is first to welcome them, to 'own' them. Let them fester away inside you during the pre-game build-up, knowing that this is just Napoleon explaining to Siggy the importance of succeeding in the challenge you are about to embark upon. The trick is not to suppress or fight those feelings, but to package them into a conscious message from Napoleon to Siggy.

The way to package and harness the power of your fear of failure is by spending the pre-game and warm-up period mentally rehearsing all the things that you expect to be called on to perform in the course of the match. It's a matter of repeating all those visualisation exercises you've built into your daily mental training routine. In effect, you're reminding Siggy that these are the particular skill files he's about to have to draw upon, and to have them ready to hand.

At the same time as you're consciously welcoming and taking ownership of your fear of failure, and selecting your skill files, you should also be doing your breathing exercises, with the aim of relaxing your body and mind so that Siggy is in the best state to receive and absorb the messages Napoleon is sending. Remember that relaxation slows down the pattern of brain waves, and the slower they are the more aware Napoleon becomes and the more responsive Siggy will be.

Visualise your first and most important game-time trigger as being the kickoff. See yourself switching Napoleon and the butterflies off, and turning everything over to Siggy, at the moment the kicker's foot strikes the ball to start the match. See and feel in advance all your fears melting away at that instant as you cut Napoleon out of the loop. See and feel yourself switching Napoleon on and off thereafter as you need him, during the lulls in the game, to exercise awareness and to pump all that pure and uncluttered data about the progress of the game into Siggy.

Pain

For the purposes of this discussion, which examines pain in the context of rugby, we'll avoid trying to draw distinctions between physical and emotional pain, beyond recognising that physical pain arises from physical contact and exertion, and emotional pain is the result of losing, of failure. We can justify this by asserting that all pain feels pretty much the same to Napoleon, and Siggy can't tell the difference anyway.

Pain is as much a part of life and rugby as is pleasure, and its very existence implies that endurance in the face of it is an essential life-skill. The trick is to make pain endurable, and the first step towards that is understanding, as far as possible, the way it works—its mechanisms. This will help us to 'own' our pain, just as we have to 'own' our fear, because we can't manage something we're in denial of.

Western medicine breaks pain down into two varieties, acute and chronic. Acute pain is that precipitated by injury, and it goes away as and when you recover. Chronic pain is the sort that sticks around, as if it's got a life of its own, after the injury itself has apparently healed, or when there's no apparent trace of physical damage.

Management of chronic pain is a medical specialty in itself and beyond the scope of the present discussion. We'll confine ourselves to looking at the management of acute pain only, on the assumption that it will go away once the injury comes right.

Nerve endings, found in nearly every tissue of the body, are the sense organs that first pick up pain signals from, say, a shoulder injured in a tackle. The signals are transmitted along the nerve cells (also called fibres) to a region in the spinal cord called the dorsal horn. This collection of nerve cells passes the information onto tracts that travel on up the spinal cord and mostly end in the thalamus, a part of the brain.

The pain signals are passed like a rugby ball along a backline, with the thalamus distributing them to their various other destinations in the brain, including the cerebral cortex, the brain's outer layer that comprises our consciousness. These cortical receiving areas seem to be where the pain signals and some of their emotional baggage get sorted into perceptions (though perception can also occur without the cortex being involved).

Other types of pain signals, such as those for intestinal colic, travel along similar pathways, taking time out to trigger nausea and vomiting reflexes on the way. (This is the source of the sensations we call the 'butterflies' and the 'screaming willies'.)

A peculiar thing about the pathway that pain travels along is that it's a two-way street: not only do pain signals pass from the damaged area to the brain, but pain-inhibiting signals also travel in the opposite direction—from the brain towards the damaged area. Somewhere within the central nervous system the opposing signals meet and, to vastly varying degrees, more or less cancel each other out.

Some pain-inhibiting signals from the brain can be triggered by such simple actions as rubbing or shaking the injured area, which alone may reduce the perception of pain enough to make it manageable. In extreme cases, such as that of soldiers wounded in the heat of battle, these automatic pain-inhibiting signals may be so strong that they mask the pain completely until the battle is over—a phenomenon called 'stress analgesia'.

Medical science is unsure exactly where it is along the nerve pathways that the pain signals and the painkiller signals actually meet. What they do know is that a range of external chemical painkillers—analgesics—can be administered to inhibit the transmission and perception of pain in the central nervous system. The best-known of these analgesics is morphine, which acts locally at the site of the injury, more generally in the dorsal horn area of the spinal cord, and within the brain itself.

The way such analgesics work in the dorsal horn led scientists to formulate the 'gateway control theory of pain', which is about as close to an understanding of the mechanism as they've so far reached. The basic principle of this theory is that the use of analgesics like morphine 'closes the gate' on the incoming pain signals, thereby preventing most or all of the pain from registering in the brain.

We can get an idea of the way the gateway mechanism works by putting it in the context of an incident writ large in New Zealand rugby lore. This was the occasion when the great lock forward, Colin Meads, was discovered to have played much of a test match against South Africa with a broken arm. In the normal course of events, a broken limb should cause so much pain that the player simply could not continue, no matter how tough he thought he was. But Meads was famous as much for his commitment—the antidote, if you like, to his fear of failure—as for his strength and skill, and he played the whole game out barely aware of the extent of the damage he had suffered.

Somewhere within Meads' brain and spinal cord, natural chemicals called 'opioid peptides' were produced which, because they work in a similar way to morphine, are often referred to as 'the body's own morphine'. According to the gateway theory, which was devised about the time this incident occurred, Meads' commitment, his mental focus, was such that the cortex of his brain generated enough opioid peptides to mask the pain of his broken limb till the final whistle. With the game behind him, and his pulse and breathing back to normal, the opioid peptides receded, and the great man felt very sore indeed.

All of which raises the question of whether we can control the pain of rugby injuries by generating those opioid peptides at will. To which the short answer is, 'Yes—at least to some degree.'

There is plenty of anecdotal evidence of pain control by auto-suggestion, which is where your Napoleon tells your Siggy that the pain you feel doesn't really exist, in the expectation that Siggy will believe him and the pain will go away. It works all right, though the degree to which it does varies hugely from one individual to the next.

However, Western medical science cannot as yet offer any set or guaranteed formula for releasing opioid peptides to inhibit all pain on demand. The only sure-fire means of on-demand pain relief are analgesics—everything, that is, from aspirin and morphine to general anaesthetic—as well as acupuncture, surgery and physical therapy.

That said, there are psychological methods of pain management —endorsed, if not yet fully understood, by medical science—which complement the standard 'RICE' formula for immediate treatment of sports injuries. RICE stands for **R**esting the injured area for 24 to 48 hours; applying **I**ce to it for 5 to 20 minutes every hour until the heat is gone from it; **C**ompressing the area with elastic bandages for 30 minutes at a time with a 15-minute spell in between; and **E**levating the injured area to help reduce swelling.

As well as physiological factors—such as the impact in a tackle—sports injury pain is made up of psychological elements, of which anxiety, fatigue and depression are the most common. This means the degree to which a rugby injury hurts is a factor of your mental state as well as of the severity of the injury. For example, a professional rugby player will feel a lot more pain from a given injury if he knows it's going to threaten his lifestyle by putting him out of a job. In this sense, pain in the wallet can contribute significantly to the pain caused by the injury itself. It comes down to the degree of pain being a factor of your awareness of it—and, since awareness is the specialist area of our friend Napoleon, we can get him to do something about it.

The two most widely accepted psychological techniques of pain relief that you can apply yourself, without expert assistance, are relaxation and imagery—and inevitably the two are closely linked.

Given that stress and tension increase the amount of pain we feel, it stands to reason that those relaxation techniques we covered in Chapter 9 will, on their own, reduce the feeling of pain, and they're especially useful immediately after the injury has occurred. Later, the imagery technique described below can be incorporated into your ongoing pain management system as well.

Let's say you're in a heap in the middle of the pitch waiting for the trainer or medics—'the zambucks', in New Zealand parlance—to arrive after pranging your shoulder in that tackle. Get yourself sitting upright if you can, and begin to focus immediately on relaxing your whole body by employing the breathing techniques described in Chapter 9. Since you were probably in a state of oxygen debt at the time the injury occurred, and because the injury itself might trigger a gasping or panting reflex, breath control immediately following an injury can be hard to achieve. But that's no bad thing in itself, because the harder it is to bring your breathing under control, the more likely the exercise is to distract your brain from its perceptions of the pain in your shoulder. Tension—muscular or mental—heightens the perception of pain, so bringing yourself into a relaxed state as soon as possible after the injury occurs is the first step towards managing injury pain. Gently shaking or rubbing the injured area helps too. After you've scraped yourself off the pitch, maintain your focus on slow, deep breathing to the deliberate exclusion, as far as possible, of the pain itself.

Once the injury has received the standard RICE treatment mentioned above, and any other remedies the zambucks might prescribe, the pain will have settled into its medium-term recovery levels. Now is the time to employ the other psychological pain management technique, imagery.

This is pure visualisation, and it goes right to core of the relationship between Siggy and Napoleon, and the principles on which this book is based. Essentially you use your imagination to transport yourself away from your pain-filled environment to a painless one. Like all the techniques described in this book, it contains elements of self-hypnosis, so the more you practise imagery the more effective it'll be. It's a technique you can eventually employ anywhere, anytime. Here's how you go about it.

Start out in a comfy chair or bed with the lights dimmed, and with no danger of interruption. Having got as comfortable as possible, start to regulate your breathing so that it's slow and full. Slowly fill your lungs up with as much air as you can take in, then just as slowly release it till it's all gone and it feels like your tummy is flapping against your backbone. Repeat this about a dozen times, or until your breathing pattern has slowed right down into a comfortable but minimal activity.

Now start to imagine yourself in your favourite scene of compelling peace and tranquillity. It may be at the beach with fluffy clouds floating overhead, the warm sun caressing you, and the little waves rustling along the shore. Now gradually introduce a sensation, such as warmth or coolness, to the area that the pain emanates from. Feel the sensation slowly beginning to swamp, to overpower, to replace the pain. Feel the pain being squeezed out, as though it were a liquid, by these ever-expanding pleasant sensations. Then concentrate on enjoying, luxuriating in them.

An alternative approach, once you've settled your breathing, is to imagine your pain as a knife stuck in the area that's hurting, and then see yourself gradually pulling it out. Feel the knife taking the pain with it as you withdraw it, and luxuriate in its absence after it's gone.

Again, it's important to remember that autosuggestion of all kinds is a skill. You're not born with it. You have to develop it. And the better you become at it, the more effective it will be in helping you manage your pain. Practised in the context of the mental training techniques described in the book, it will become a very effective method of pain relief indeed.

– 14 –
Playing the mind-game

> The highest possible stage in moral culture is when we recognise that we ought to control our thoughts.
> CHARLES DARWIN

The key to performing to your potential on the rugby field lies in playing the game beforehand in your mind. This involves loading the hard disk—the permanent memory—of your personal in-built computer, your Siggy, with all the skills and options most appropriate to the position you play.

This preprogramming has the effect of ensuring that Siggy has all the relevant skill files at his fingertips, ready to be put to use when Napoleon feeds in all that pure and uncluttered information that he's gathering by way of the five senses. Having those skill files all primed and ready not only shaves vital fractions of a second off the time Siggy takes to access the right file for a given situation, but it also reduces—or even eliminates—the danger of Napoleon trying to tell Siggy which particular file to pull out. Once you've got all the options stored on his hard disk, you can leave it to Siggy to decide which skill file to activate in any given circumstance.

This preprogramming is achieved physically by practice, and it's achieved mentally by visualisation. You could go so far as to say that practice and visualisation achieve the same goal—the preprogramming of Siggy's hard disk with relevant skill files. Skill practice consists of physical repetition within physical space, while skill-filing is performed by visualisation within the cyberspace of the mind.

Just as the physical practice required for rugby varies between the fifteen different playing positions on the field, so the visualisation exercises must also be tailored to suit: the fly half's visualisation practice session is quite different from the lock's; the fullback's from the hooker's.

In this chapter we analyse the various playing positions so that you know what to incorporate into the visualisation exercises that are a key element, along with goal-setting and affirmation, of mind-training for rugby football. The following analysis can also be useful in helping you write affirmations, but it's primarily geared to help you create mental pictures of yourself performing on the field.

As we have already learned, the visualisation exercise can be carried out anywhere, any time you get the opportunity to close your eyes and block out the rest of the world. But the best time is just before you go to sleep: you can be sure that Siggy will be weaving those skill files through the cyberspace of your dreams all the time you're unconscious, because they were the last deliberate thoughts fed into him before you and Napoleon switched off for the night.

The fifteen rugby union positions break down naturally into two groups: forwards and backs. In turn, both these groups have skill-file demands that break down into a further three subsets.

For backs the three skill-file subsets are attack, defence and kicking.

For forwards the three subsets are attack, defence and set-play.

There is a further skill-file subset that applies to all forwards; this subset covers the pick-and-go and ball-protection options.

The way to use the analysis is first to locate your own position among the fifteen (or twelve, actually, since we don't distinguish between the respective skill-file requirements of the two wings, the two locks, or the two props). Then, in turn, work your way through each of the three sub-groups, seeing yourself in your mind's eye performing the required skills. If you are a forward, add the pick-and-go and ball-protection options.

Make the imaginary performance of the skills as realistic as you possibly can. Try to imagine what the ball actually feels like to catch, how your body feels as you set yourself up for your famous winger's sidestep, or how your propping shoulders love the impact of powering into a maul or over your tackled team-mate to protect the ball possession.

You've got five senses, so try to work them all into your visualisation. Obviously sight and touch are the two most important, but try to imagine the sounds of the game, the smells of the game, the taste that comes into your mouth during the game—remembering all the while that nothing tastes as sweet as a difficult skill superbly performed.

The skills listed below cover the core demands of each position, but not necessarily in order of priority. Set up your own personal visualisation programme by taking into account your own personal skill strengths (and the correction of weaknesses), the demands of the coach and the strategy of the team. The latter two are frequently one and the same. If the coach is moaning about your team's lousy defence last Saturday, you could make tackling the main focus of the defensive segment of your visualisation exercises. If he's demanding more of the go-forward with the ball in hand, crank up the supercharger technique described earlier. If you've been knocking the ball on at pick-and-go opportunities, your visualisation could include seeing, feeling, tasting, smelling and hearing yourself picking up the ball cleanly when it's laid back for you.

Work out your own set of priorities.

So here we go with the core skill files that have to be developed by visualisation for each position.

The backs

The fullback

As an attacker. He injects himself into the backline on either the open or the blind side, from either set- or phase-play, generally with the idea of setting up his wings by punching holes in the opposing line. He counterattacks by bringing the ball back into the backline from defensive positions.

As a defender. As the last line of defence, his tackling skills have to be of the highest quality, especially in one-on-one situations. Recognising that the ball-carrier has the advantage in the one-on-one scenario, he must be aware of positioning himself to narrow the ball-carrier's options, to squeeze him into the most vulnerable angle possible to effect the tackle. His catching skills have to be meticulous, especially under the high ball.

As a kicker. First and foremost, he's there to relieve pressure with long line-kicks, with the absolute priority being to find touch. He must also have a capacity to counterattack by way of the kick, using the long and high punt for position and to embarrass the opposing defence, or the short chip and grubber from which possession can be regained after finding space behind the opposing defence.

The wings

As attackers. They are primarily finishers, the try-scorers at the end of the chain, the players that the other fourteen have manoeuvred into a position to score. They can also come off their blind sides to be injected as decoys or ball-carriers anywhere along the backline, including outside the other winger. Speed and elusiveness are key elements, with pure power as a back-up. Their other attacking requirements duplicate and overlap those of the fullback.

As defenders. They face similar demands to those of the fullback, frequently finding themselves as the last line of defence, so their tackling has to be good. They also have a vital role as cover defenders, especially coming off their blind side as back-up for the whole of the backline, including their fellow winger way over on the other side of the pitch.

As kickers. They have both defensive and attacking kicking capabilities; the chip-and-chase is a key weapon in their armoury, as is the touch-finder on defence. They must also be adept at long-range positioning punts because, like the fullback, they often take part in aerial ping-pong matches with their opposites.

The centre

As an attacker. His key role is to try to get his wings away. He's a superb timer of the pass; he may need to be a line-buster and/or a ball distributor, depending on the skill-set of his second five-eighth (inside centre); he's charged with getting the ball over the advantage line, providing the go-forward, retaining and recycling possession. He often shares or swaps these roles with the second five-eighth, who may be a stepper, elusive off either foot. The centre is often the one who sets up the target-play.

As a defender. He, along with his second five-eighth partner, is the mid-field defensive screen in charge of a wide zone both inside and outside of his own position, whether the defensive style be man-on-man, drift, one-out, or cover. He's the big-hit tackler out to force the turnover. As with his attacking, his defensive roles are often interchangeable with those of the second five-eighth.

As a kicker. He's generally the least used in this role of any of the backs, but he still needs to be competent at line-kicking, and able to pull a chip or grubber kick out of his bag of tricks when the occasion demands.

The second five-eighth (inside centre)

As an attacker. He may need to be a stepper and a ball distributor, depending on the skill-set of his centre partner, so he may need to be able to beat his opponent one-on-one off either foot, as well as being a master of the weighted and timed pass. He works in close partnership with the centre outside him and, like the centre, may be called on to perform as a line-buster; his skills and those of the centre are sometimes interchangeable.

As a defender. Tackling is his forte; ideally he'll have the capacity to deliver the king-hit, but he has to be technically good whether he is big or small. His target is seldom the opposing second five-eighth, but is more likely to be someone further out in the backline. He's the one who most often nails the opposing centre and he runs cover for his own outside backs.

As a kicker. The requirements are pretty much the same as those for the centre, but he may be called upon to use his kicking options more often, especially the defensive ones. He needs to have a chip and a grubber kick to supplement his stepping on attack.

The first five-eighth (fly half)

As an attacker. He needs to be able to run and step a little, if only to keep the opposition's inside backs honest, but he's primarily a ball distributor and play-maker; he chooses the options, deals the cards.

He's got hands like glue, can pass inside or outside, long or short, vary the angle of attack, or hand-off to a forward or another back coming through on either side. His essential goal is to create opportunities to breach the opposition's advantage line, either close in or out wide.

As a defender. This used to be a relatively minor role but it is assuming increasing importance in the modern game, so he has to be an effective tackler. Because he tends to be of smaller build and is confronting big forwards, he has to have good technique. He also has an expanding role as a cover defender for the backs outside him.

As a kicker. Kicking is strongly emphasised in the fly half's game because, if anyone gets to kick, he's usually the first to have that option. He has to have the full armoury of kicking skills, from chips and bombs to grubbers, box kicks, wipers and line kicks; he's also usually the goal kicker, and the restarter from the twenty-two and halfway.

The halfback (scrum half)

As an attacker. He is becoming more of a runner, a gap-spotter, these days, but just as there is an emphasis on kicking for the fly half, the scrum half's emphasis is on passing. He is the link between the forwards and the backs, which is why in New Zealand they refer to him as half-a-back. He's also the director of the forward pack, steering the tight five like a bulldozer driver to where they'll be most effective.

As a defender. He has a major role in close-in defending these days, especially round set-play, rucks and mauls, so his tackling skills have to be impeccable. He also has an expanding role as a cover defender.

As a kicker. This is a particularly specialised role because much of the kicking is done under pressure, typically from behind set-play, rucks or mauls, with opposing loose forwards converging. The standard options are the box kick, and the deeper kick for position, but line-kicking is also important because the halfback has an advantage over his first five-eighth in already being 10 metres further up-field when he kicks; the grubber kick, especially down the tramlines on the blind side, is also a halfback specialty.

The forwards

The number eight (back-rower)

As an attacker. He has the crucial role of controlling possession at the base of the scrum, and preparing a safe delivery channel to the halfback. He's also the key hitter-upper, getting the ball over the advantage line to start the rest of the pack on the go-forward; he's second only to the open-side flanker in getting to the breakdown on the open side, firstly to secure possession, then to rekindle the forward momentum. He is also called on often as a passer, mostly to the halfback but sometimes directly to the first-five, depending on the option chosen.

As a defender. He ranges across the whole gamut of defensive zones, from close in to the set-play and closing holes in the line-out, to policing the fringes of the rucks and mauls, to covering way out behind the backline. He tackles a lot, and from every conceivable angle; he also fields a lot of loose ball and high kicks, so his handling has to be impeccable. He's especially conscious of protecting his halfback and first five-eighth from the opposing loose forwards.

As a set-player. He's the last man down in the scrum, locking the locks into place and delivering his own fair share of the grunt. He's a key figure in the line-out, often roaming the length of it, whether the throw-in be his own team's or the opposition's, and he can be called on either to lift or to jump. He is most often the player who receives the deeper kickoff, and brings the ball up from the shorter ones once a ruck or maul is formed. He is often put in position to receive a pass as a runner off the ruck or maul.

The open-side flanker

As an attacker. He's the first to the scene of the breakdown, especially on the open side, securing possession and setting up the retain-and-recycle phase for the other forwards coming in behind him. He also serves as a link with the backs, passing them into an attack phase after recovering the ball from the breakdown. He has a growing role taking hand-offs from the halfback or first five-eighth and forcing his way over the advantage line.

As a defender. He's the consummate tackler, taking the first tackle round his side of the scrum, ruck or maul. It's also his job to harry the opposition's inside backs, and one of the best services he can render his team is in bringing down the opposing ball-carrier behind their advantage line, then setting up the go-forward for his own pack.

As a set-player. He has a role both in pushing at the scrums and providing a lateral force against the nearer lock to keep the scrum straight and its power centred. He may do a bit of jumping or lifting, but he's usually the tail-gunner in the line-outs, with his sights set firmly on the opposition's inside backs. When receiving kickoffs, he stands fairly near the middle of the field, just on his own side of the 10-metre line, tidying up at the resultant ruck or maul if he has to.

The blind-side flanker

As an attacker. Often the bigger of the two flankers, he's frequently involved in the planned moves, and gets to run the ball at the opposition, especially from set-play and hand-offs, or to pass directly to the inside backs. He's the first to the breakdown on the blind side, and third to it (after the open-side flanker and the number eight) on the open side. His skills are often interchangeable with those of the number eight and, increasingly, with those of the locks.

As a defender. He is first to the tackle round the blind side from both set and broken play, and he's got a major role to play in cover-defending for his backs. He does a lot of tidying up of broken play, and he's the key to getting his open-side flanker and number eight going forward after they've reached the breakdown.

As a set-player. He's got the same role in the scrum as his open-side partner. He's generally second from the back of the line-out and, as such, has roles as both a lifter and a jumper. He helps create a two-pronged cover defence off the back of the line-out by following the same trail blazed by the open-side flanker. When receiving the kickoff, he stands between the locks and the open-side flanker, to help with the short and nudge kickoffs which are coming into the game more often. He's a bit of a sweeper for the in-field receiving lock.

The locks

As attackers. They have got the not-very-glamorous role of providing the big go-forward momentum by being the hammer that drives in the set-up nail of the loose forwards at rucks and mauls. These days they're also increasingly getting to run with the ball in short bursts which demand explosive power and speed.

As defenders. Their prime role is as drivers, to stop, and then to reverse, the opposition pack's forward momentum at rucks and mauls, but increasingly they're being called on for close-in tackling as well.

As set-players. The tallest and often the heaviest in the team, they are the power base of the scrum and the principal jumpers in the line-out. They play a fundamental role in receiving short kickoffs, from in-field and touchline positions respectively; on their own kickoffs, they're the main means of getting the ball back by way of the clean take or knock-back, especially on the short kickoff.

The props

As attackers. They have the same roles as the locks.

As defenders. They have the same roles as the locks.

As set-players. They are the foundation of the scrum at the tight and loose head respectively; if they fold, so will the scrum. Their scrummaging roles call for a combination of precise and refined technique, plus explosive power. In the line-outs they are called on to serve primarily as lifters and blockers, but they may also get to do a bit of jumping, especially at the front. At the kickoff, they serve as the support player for each lock, lifting the locks to receive, or running onto the ball once the locks have secured possession at their own kickoffs.

The hooker

As an attacker. He has got a multifaceted role, but primarily he's there to build on the go-forward momentum initiated by the locks and the props. If the locks and the props have created the momentum before he gets there though, he can look around for opportunities to embarrass and intimidate the opposition backs by showing up in unexpected places anywhere along his own backline.

As a defender. His roles are the same as those of the locks and props.

As a set-player. He has the vital role of throwing the ball into the line-out and, as any lock will tell you, catching the thing is easy—it's getting the hooker's aim right that's the hard part. Hooking the ball in the scrum involves a lot less skill, but conceding a tight head is even more embarrassing to the hooker than missing his jumper on the line-out throw-in. The hooker is also expected to be the mortar in the scrum foundation between the brick-like props, and to be able to shove as well as hook the ball from the feed. Receiving the kick-off, he will occasionally have to take a long ball, but is essentially a sweeper for the locks, and especially for the touchline lock.

All forwards

Pick-and-go and ball-protection options. When running onto the held-up or tackled ball, all forwards face the options of picking the ball up and going ahead with it (the pick-and-go) or getting in front of the ball to shield it for their other forwards yet to arrive. Getting in front of the ball is the default option—the one you automatically resort to—but when the opposition's defensive line is stretched close in to the ruck, maul or tackle, that's the time to pick-and-go.

– 15 –
Of gamesmanship and things . . .

> You have no idea what a poor opinion I have of myself
> —and how little I deserve it.
>
> **W.S. GILBERT**

At the start of this book, we drew parallels between contact sports and warfare, going so far as to suggest that modern sports, and particularly the contact ones, may be civilisation's substitute for military adventuring, now that the news media and weapons of mass destruction have taken the romance out of old-style killing wars. If that's the case, and this being a book about psychological training, it's appropriate that we look at the role of psychological warfare in the context of the rugby codes. Of course, in sport it's not referred to as psychological warfare—instead it's called gamesmanship.

Everything we've looked at so far in this book has been aimed at getting the best possible game out of ourselves, through mental (psychological) training. Gamesmanship is the skill of putting your opponents off their game—getting them to play below their potential—by getting their Napoleons to send muddy, cluttered, or plain wrong information to their Siggys.

Gamesmanship is a legitimate competitive device with potentially devastating effects, though not necessarily upon the intended target. In noncontact sports, competitors who employ gamesmanship—we call them gamers—have to confine themselves to tricks of suggestion and disruption, but in contact sports the range of legitimate gamesmanship devices extends to intimidation and provocation.

Gamesmanship is part and parcel of sport, but most top sportspeople don't consciously bother with it; instead they rely on constant improvement of their own performance to bring them success, rather than undermining that of their opponents. No sportsperson ever exhausts their capacity for improvement, and most regard gamesmanship as an unnecessary distraction from their central purpose: to succeed through constant improvement.

Gamesmanship is by no means an indispensable weapon in the armoury of the successful rugby player. That's because it has the potential to be self-deluding, is at least as likely to have a negative impact on the gamer as on the opponent, and it's relatively easy to become immune to. And there's another downside to gamesmanship in the context of a contact sport: success at it may come at the cost of physical hurt to the gamer.

Arguably the best and most famous gamer in modern rugby union was the All Black captain of the 1990s, Sean Fitzpatrick. From the hooker's position at the rugby coalface, Fitzpatrick employed all the gamer's skills on virtually every team—and referee—he came across. His constant patter and niggling inevitably drew retribution from its targets, and Fitzpatrick emerged from one test with a set of South African teeth marks in his ear.

That particular incident was a triumph of Fitzpatrick's skill as a gamer: by losing his cool and sinking his teeth into the All Black captain, the South African player effectively conceded that Fitzpatrick had got the better of him, and both his and his team's performance fell to pieces thereafter. The incident shattered the reigning world champion side's aura of invincibility, and precipitated a form slump that lasted right through the next world championship tournament.

Fitzpatrick undoubtedly felt that teeth marks in his ear were a small price to pay for the collapse of the Springboks' concentration. But it was a price just the same—the price of gamesmanship in a contact sport. If you're going to be a gamer, your success will be measured to some degree by whether or not you manage to provoke your opponent(s) into illegal action. And successful provocation in rugby can precipitate far worse retribution than a chewed ear.

This is by no means to suggest that such reactions are justified. Of course they're not. But if you're going to practise gamesmanship in a physical contact sport, you have to expect to pay a physical contact price for being good at it.

Gamesmanship will always be a popular device among those with the temperament and taste for it, and no player can survive at the top levels of rugby without at least an understanding of its principles, if only to recognise them when the opposition resorts to them.

The essential thing to remember about gamesmanship is that it works only if the target falls for it—and if the target *doesn't* fall for it, the gamer then has to deal with the psychological effect of being deprived of a weapon. A competitor with a habitual reliance on gamesmanship is vulnerable to an opponent who sees through the device and declines to be affected by it.

Gamesmanship is thus a double-edged sword, with the potential to be as much a liability as an asset. Skill and concentration will always have the capacity to thwart gamesmanship, whatever the game.

Gamesmanship is the art of suggestion. The gamer relies on the opponent taking up the suggestion and performing to its implicitly lowered expectations.

Gamesmanship is based on an understanding of the interaction between Siggy, your in-built computer, and Napoleon, your in-built computer operator. The way it works is that you suggest to your opponent's Napoleon that the game is stacked against him, that he's not up to the task he faces, and you rely on the opponent to pass this perception on to his Siggy, who delivers accordingly. The more the opponent takes aboard the negative suggestions fed to him by the gamer, the more muddied and cluttered the information his Napoleon passes on to his Siggy, so the worse he plays. It's as simple as that.

Later in this chapter we'll look at strategies for making ourselves immune to gamesmanship, but first it helps to be aware of the main games that gamers play.

A typical tactic of the gamer is commiseration—sympathising with the opponent over the difficult situation he's been placed in by the gamer. The intent is to introduce the opponent's Napoleon to the idea that he's battling against some element other than the playing skill of the gamer. The other element may be bad luck, bad weather, a bad surface, an unsympathetic referee, incompetent fellow team members, or whatever. The message is that the gamer himself is somehow immune to these negative effects, while the opponent is vulnerable to them.

A second device of the gamer is gratitude: he thanks his opponent for making things easier for him, as if that was the opponent's intention. This is a bit more subtle, but no less detectable, than the sympathy act. The subtlety lies in the fact that the gamer flatters his opponent, tells him nice things about himself, suggests he's an oh-so-decent guy for playing into the gamer's grateful hands.

A third device is the barefaced lie: the gamer says of his opponent's ground-gobbling line kick, 'That doesn't do you any good', though they both know it has. No sophisticated gamer resorts to the lie because it's rare to find a target dumb enough to be negatively—rather than positively—affected by it. But the lie is still a legitimate device, and there are people so lacking in confidence in their own judgement that they can be put off their game by it.

Much more widespread and effective is the technique of disruption, the purpose of which is to prevent the target settling into his game and getting a rhythm going. Techniques range from slowing down or speeding up the game, to acts of minor irritation, like dropping the ball just out of reach of the opposing halfback when he's trying to get hold of it to feed the scrum.

In a contact sport like rugby, there are also those other two gaming devices that you need to be aware of: intimidation and provocation. They work exactly the same way as commiseration and gratitude—that is, by using the power of suggestion—but they do so in the context of physical danger and the fear it can arouse.

In Chapter 13 we analysed the mechanism of fear, saw how useful it is, and how to turn it to our advantage. Intimidation is aimed at triggering this fear in the target player in the hope he won't be able to organise and channel it constructively. The first step in doing this is to let him know you've singled him out as your target, and eye contact is the primary way of starting this communication. Picking a target out to run the ball at is another, while many intimidatory messages can be communicated in the tackle.

Gamesmanship is dependent on two-way communication, which is usually begun by eye contact. If the target declines to meet the gamer's eye, he'll have to fall back on vocal and body language to reveal his intention.

As with intimidation, so too with provocation, which usually requires verbal communication: unless the gamer can communicate it precisely by way of body language or eye contact—not always easy—he is reduced to letting the target player know verbally how he wants him to react, which he does at his peril. The gamer's aim is to wreck his opponent's game by making him lose concentration and retaliate in an illegal manner (such as munching on his ear). To do this he attacks his target's self-esteem with methods that range from name-calling to derogatory remarks about physical appearance or even sexuality.

Sound a bit pathetic? It tends to be, and it needn't bother you, but it remains a legitimate gamesmanship device, and it's extraordinary the number of mugs who repeatedly fall for it.

Developing gaming skills takes time, though some people are born to it. It's essentially acting, and the only convincing actors are those who live the part they're playing. This requires the ability to live not only 'in the now', but also 'in the then' or 'in the maybe'. As an exercise, it's essentially schizophrenic, which is why it's as potentially dangerous to the gamer as to the target. Some people are cut out for it, some can cut themselves out for it, and some will never be any good at it no matter how hard they try. The only way to see if it offers any potential for improving your own performance is to try it out, while understanding that you don't have to be a good gamer to be a good rugby player.

Start by picking out your opposite in the other team by eye contact, then try the sympathy and gratitude lines on him, perhaps by praising him up for something he's obviously not that flash at. 'Great tackle,' you tell him admiringly, after he's just barely managed to scrag you to the ground instead of nailing you with the king-hit you thought he was in a position to deliver. Your aim is to seduce him into a confused state of mind where he's more amenable to your Napoleon's suggestions than he is to his own. Aim at replacing his Napoleon's messages with yours. Interpret every development in the game in the light of what's bad for him and what's good for you.

Back up the verbal suggestions with supportive body language.

Stifle a giggle if he does something constructive. Shake your head sadly—for him, not for you—when, say, he succeeds in tidying up a bit of possession from broken play. Be yawningly casual when you burgle possession from his team—after all, it's only to be expected that you can get hold of the ball whenever you want to, while for him it's a rare and notable achievement.

Move on into intimidation and provocation, if you find you've got the stomach for them. Be aware that these are more challenging elements of gamesmanship than sympathy and gratitude, because the measure of your success at them will, to some extent, result in physical damage to yourself. If that occurs, you've got to be big enough not to react illegally yourself, and to fully exploit the advantage you've gained by the target player's losing his cool.

In the famous ear-biting incident, for example, Fitzpatrick was too good a gamer to retaliate reflexively. But he made a big enough fuss to ensure the incident was not lost on the referee, the linesmen and—by way of the television cameras—the spectators. In doing so, Fitzpatrick made the outcome of his provocative gamesmanship far more devastating for the target player (who ended up being banned from the game for a period), and for his target's team, than any amount of physical retribution could have produced.

We can turn now from examining how gamers and gamesmanship work, to creating the antidote to them. And it's not difficult. To frustrate the gamer, all you have to do is ignore him, shut him out of your mind. We've seen that, to be successful, gamesmanship requires two-way communication between the gamer and the target. And if the target simply declines to communicate—either vocally or by body language (which includes eye contact)—there's nothing the gamer can do about it.

Understand that if you give your opponent free and uncluttered access to your Napoleon, he'll turn your little emperor against you. Be aware that seemingly innocent comments, gestures and eye contact may be designed to get your Napoleon active and alarmed, evaporating your expectation of success and siphoning off your confidence.

Also, understand that every action of your gaming opponent is a component of his wider game, and reveals something about him—something which is grist to the mill of your own awareness. Observe the opponent, note what he appears to be doing, and suspend judgement on it. Simply be informed.

If he's standing on his head blowing raspberries at the crowd as you step up to a line-out, file this information for processing by Siggy, who may already be holding other evidence that this is a last-resort tactic of a player who thinks the game is slipping out of his team's reach. Then forget about him, and turn responsibility for your performance at the set-play over to your Siggy. Don't say to yourself, 'My god, this guy's trying to psych me out—how the blazes do I handle that?' Just be aware, and don't be lured into making judgements about him or his antics.

You don't have to develop your own arsenal of gamesmanship ploys to defend yourself from gamers. Instead, just receive the gamer's messages as items of information about his game, refuse to respond or communicate in any conscious way, and stay non-judgemental. Receive your gaming opponent's messages as welcome information about him—information that he wouldn't otherwise be revealing—and your body will unconsciously and effortlessly give him back the message that his tactics are helping rather than hindering you. Never let him get under your skin. Never let him provoke you.

And 999 times out of 1000, that'll be enough to destroy him, because most gamers get into gamesmanship to cover up basic shortcomings in their game. That leaves just the one gamer in 1000—those rare Sean Fitzpatricks of this world—whom you've also got to beat by playing better rugby.

If, after trying the defensive exercises outlined here, you still find yourself a sucker for a good gamer—for suggestion, disruption, provocation or intimidation—the thing to do is go out of your way to watch the very best of them at work. The good gamers are easy to identify, because they all tend to get reputations for gaming. Some gamers indulge in gamesmanship precisely because they hunger for the gamer's reputation—which in itself suggests an underlying vulnerability.

Seek the good gamers out, expect to be entertained, and turn your Napoleon loose on them from the sideline or from behind the video remote. Watch everything they do, and put it all in the perspective of their immediate goal, which is to feed damaging information or perceptions into the opponent's Napoleon.

Remember, the gamer has a right to resort to gamesmanship, and you must never allow yourself to feel resentful about their indulging it.

Sportsmanship

There is another and devastating antidote to gamesmanship which, depending on your temperament, may be even more effective than simply ignoring the gamer. This is the antidote of proactive sportsmanship. It involves responding to the gamer's overtures, but from the conviction that he's fundamentally well disposed towards you, and you are appreciative of that. This approach is particularly effective when the overtures are aggressive or intimidating, because a genuinely friendly or sympathetic response is frustrating and bewildering to the gamer.

The advantage of this strategy is that you can apply it to everybody you deal with, on and off the field. It can become your strategy for living. And it has the pleasant side effect of making people like and admire you. It's a case of seeing good in everybody in spite of—even because of—evidence to the contrary. And, since people tend to perform to other people's expectations, proactive sportsmanship has the capacity to make good sports of bad.

Sportsmanship is variously defined in dictionaries as exhibiting qualities 'such as fairness, generosity, observance of the rules, and good humour when losing' (Collins), to 'fair play' (Oxford), to 'chivalrous and fair-minded' behaviour by a person 'willing to incur risks, and prepared to suffer defeat in fair competition without complaining' (H.C. Wyld). But it all comes down to your own notions of what constitutes human decency. In its broadest application, that can be defined as wishing other people well. Within sport it implies playing within the rules, respecting your opponents for subjecting themselves to those same rules, being modest and non-gloating in victory, and good-humoured, generous and forgiving of yourself in defeat.

These are universal values which transcend culture, politics, religion, and all those other social and economic differences that tend to push people apart. And that's exactly what sport does: it transcends people's diversity by bringing them together under a single set of rules and values.

Contact sports like the rugby codes go one step further, creating a climate within which the aggression and violence that seem to be an intrinsic part of the human condition—and which historically have been the main agents for keeping people apart—are acknowledged, and channelled into uniting them. The ultimate lesson of rugby and contact sports may be that, when harnessed to a code of behaviour and rules that all parties subscribe to, those historically destructive traits of violence and aggression can produce a positive and constructive outcome.

And, of course, they provide a vital means through which the individual can experience the thrill of personal achievement. Which is what this book has been all about—the notion that striving is worthy, but succeeding is worthier; playing is great, but winning is best. If real life was half as simple and fair, we wouldn't need sport.

You don't necessarily have to predetermine where you fit in on the behavioural scale between gamesmanship and sportsmanship. If you follow the formulae for mental fitness outlined in this book—the goal-setting, affirmation, visualisation and all the other techniques—Napoleon and Siggy will spontaneously work out your personal place in the scheme of things. Maybe you'll be a gamer. More likely you won't. What you will find is that the adoption of a mental training regime will, of itself, release and develop your own individual character and style. Through Napoleon and Siggy you'll discover yourself. You'll revel in the experience and you may be surprised at what you find out about yourself.

So get out there and be a focused and determined winner, modest in victory, honouring your opponents whatever the outcome, and never compromising your own essential human dignity and decency. Explore your potential. See how far you can go. Enjoy your achievements. Be grateful for the knowledge that your setbacks bring. In short, organise and structure your thinking processes, then go out and enjoy the incomparable experience of playing winning rugby.